An Historian Looks at 1 Timothy 2:11–14

An Historian Looks at 1 Timothy 2:11–14

The Authentic Traditional Interpretation and Why It Disappeared

J. G. Brown

WIPF & STOCK · Eugene, Oregon

AN HISTORIAN LOOKS AT 1 TIMOTHY 2:11–14
The Authentic Traditional Interpretation and Why It Disappeared

Copyright © 2012 J. G. Brown. All rights reserved. Except for brief quotations in critical publications or reviews, no part of this book may be reproduced in any manner without prior written permission from the publisher. Write: Permissions, Wipf and Stock Publishers, 199 W. 8th Ave., Suite 3, Eugene, OR 97401.

Wipf & Stock
An Imprint of Wipf and Stock Publishers
199 W. 8th Ave., Suite 3
Eugene, OR 97401
www.wipfandstock.com

ISBN 13: 978-1-61097-600-8

Manufactured in the U.S.A.

Unless marked otherwise, all scripture references are from the NEW AMERICAN STANDARD BIBLE®. Copyright © 1960, 1962, 1963, 1968, 1971, 1972, 1973, 1975, 1977, 1995 by The Lockman Foundation. Used by permission. All rights reserved.

To
Bob

Contents

Preface ix
Introduction: Concerning Arrows and Targets xi

1 The Authentic Traditional Interpretation 1

2 The Nineteenth Century:
      "A Mingling of Heaven and Earth" 31

3 Contemporary Interpretations
      of 1 Timothy 2:11–14 52

4 Where Do We Go From Here? 66

   *Appendix: Excerpts From Luther's
      "Temporal Authority" and Calvin's* Institutes 75
   Bibliography 93

Preface

As a history teacher, I have long been aware that prior to the nineteenth century the general population applied the creation order, as they understood it in Genesis 2 and 3, to the culture at large. This mandated the subordination of women to men in the arenas of government, business, the academy, et cetera—and in the church, or so I assumed. Then, when traditionalists lost the culture wars of the nineteenth century, they jettisoned the application of creation ordinances to the civil kingdom and sought to defend what turf they had left (the church) ever more vigorously—or so I assumed. What I was not able to do was reconcile the traditional theological position with the clear connection the early women's rights movement had with evangelical revival and reform. This appeared to be evangelical Protestantism against itself and remained a conundrum until I read David VanDrunen's book, *Natural Law and the Two Kingdoms*. VanDrunen's thesis, combined with my own extensive research, led me to the discovery that all prominent exegetes prior to the nineteenth century, including Luther and Calvin, saw creation ordinances as foundational to the civil kingdom, but not to life in the church. Most churches honored creation ordinances in their ecclesiastical polity concerning men and women; however, they did not see creation ordinances as organic to the church. This not only made sense in terms of what the exegetes themselves have written, but it also provided a framework for understanding the events of the nineteenth century. I am now convinced that the authentic traditional interpretation of 1 Timothy 2:11–14 no longer exists. I have approached this study from an historical perspective and have not ventured into VanDrunen's critique of neo-Calvinism, although the two may not be completely unrelated. In any event, complementarians/hierarchists need to look anew at their arguments and the presuppositions behind those arguments. The case for male headship / female subordination *in the church* is not nearly as well anchored in Protestant theological tradition as has been assumed.

Since I have been busily engaged in the classroom, I am deeply indebted to various persons who have helped me put this research project together. First of all, I would like to thank the scholars who either encouraged me and/or pointed me in the right direction in my search for leading traditional theologians. So, thank you Jerram Barrs, Nicholas Perrin, David W. Spencer, Aida Besançon Spencer, Philip B. Payne, Barry Hamilton, Douglas Cullum, and Gregory Wills. I am also deeply indebted to Ellen Wolkensperg and Bonni Morrell for reading and critiquing my work in its early stages. The love and support of my children; friends; and former students, such as Olivia Lahman; were essential to seeing this project through to the end. Lastly, I would like to thank my husband, Bob, without whom the entire project would have floundered in a sea of computer and word processing glitches.

2 Corinthians 10:5

Introduction

Concerning Arrows and Targets

> *A woman must quietly receive instruction with all submissiveness.*[12] *But I do not allow a woman to teach or exercise authority over a man, but to remain quiet.* [13]*For it was Adam who was first created, and then Eve.* [14]*And it was not Adam who was first deceived, but the woman being deceived, fell into transgression.* (1 Tim 2:11-14, NASB)

ONCE UPON a time a nobleman rode into the forest to practice his archery skills. He had not gone far when he began to notice a series of targets painted on various trees. Someone had shot an arrow into the exact center of each target. The nobleman was very impressed with such talent and consequently sent his men in search of the unknown archer. After some time, the men learned that the archer for whom they were searching was but a lad. They found the boy and brought him to the nobleman, who immediately asked him the secret of his extraordinary skill. The boy quickly responded, "That's easy. First I shoot the arrows; then I paint the targets."

No story better illustrates many of the attempts to interpret and apply the 1 Timothy 2: 11–14 passage over the last one hundred and fifty years. The problem of allowing desired outcomes to dictate evidence exists across the board, but is especially egregious among those who claim to uphold a "traditional" exegesis. This monograph is a humble attempt to bring greater clarity to the authentic traditional interpretation of this passage, as well as to why it disappeared, and to explore how the true historic interpretation stands up against accusations that Christianity has been a bulwark of patriarchy in the modern world.

Theologians have not been the only ones shooting arrows and then painting targets. Secular historians, through textbooks and in the classroom, have played no small part in sowing the seeds of doubt and skepticism that characterize our culture today. They often portray Christianity as the primary source of bloody crusades, witch-hunts, patriarchal domination, imperialism, and other crimes against humanity. The following quote concerning Reformation-era women is taken from a widely used world history textbook and illustrates the point:

> The Reformers appealed to religious sentiments, but political and social agendas inspired many who joined them. Part of the appeal of Lutheranism to German-speakers was in reaction to the power of Italians in the Catholic church. Peasants and urban laborers sometimes defied their masters by adopting a different faith. Neither tradition had a special attraction for women, since both Protestants and Roman Catholics believed in male dominance in the church and family.[1]

1. Bulliet et al., *The Earth and Its Peoples*, 447.

The elevated status of women in Western civilization is truly an historical anomaly. So, if Christianity was not a primary source of this elevated status, what was? I have asked this question and have come full circle—back to Christianity, particularly the Protestant Reformation and its emphasis on the priesthood of all believers. The Reformation doctrine of the priesthood of all believers was like a stone thrown into the center of a tranquil pond. Over the centuries this doctrine had a ripple effect on churches first, and eventually on social and political institutions. By the nineteenth century the continuing rise of religious individualism became the great liberator of ordinary women in the English-speaking world. While keeping all this in mind, my primary purpose here is to explore the charge against Christianity of male domination by looking at one of the few New Testament passages that might be interpreted to promote just that.

The legacy of Christianity is indeed a curious thing—upholding hierarchies and patriarchal assumptions on the one hand, and on the other hand, topping these age-old structures with egalitarian doctrines, such as the priesthood of all believers. Do we simply acquiesce to the idea that the Bible can be used to support anything, or is there a coherent historical and theological framework for better understanding this paradox? I would contend for the latter. One key to solving this puzzle lies in understanding pre-nineteenth-century assumptions concerning the relationship between the temporal and spiritual kingdoms. The population in general, including most prominent Bible commentators, believed that the creation order was foundational to civil authority, but not necessarily to the church. This assumption also characterized the authentic traditional interpretation of 1 Timothy 2:11–14.

It is commonly acknowledged that the emancipation of women in the Western world was closely associated with events in the late eighteenth and early nineteenth centuries. It was a time of great humanitarian reform, ranging from prison reform to the abolition of slavery to women's rights and much more. As I read the arguments for and against giving women a more expansive role in shaping social and political institutions, I naturally encountered biblical arguments on both sides of the debate. Paul's words in 1 Timothy 2: 11–14 were often alluded to or referenced explicitly. Furthermore, because the strictures these verses place on women are grounded in creation, traditionalists considered them authoritative in the culture at large. That was an assumption based on centuries of Christian thought concerning natural law (including creation ordinances) and the relationship of Christians to civil society and the state. Consequently, I formed the following hypothesis: Although the early women's rights movement was animated by broad Protestant convictions that God dwells within the individual soul and that all persons are equal in his eyes, exegetical support for the subjugation of women to men in civil society was grounded in natural law/creation ordinances as expounded in 1 Timothy 2 and therefore normative for all times and places. In addition, I expected to see at least some ambiguity expressed by Bible commentators who recognized the spiritual nature of the kingdom of Christ and how the Holy Spirit might empower women in the church in ways the culture did not.

I set up my research to investigate the following questions: How have leading Bible commentators, representing the various Protestant traditions since the Reformation, interpreted 1 Timothy 2:11–14, and are any patterns discernable? Are there timeless principles that emerge from this passage, or do interpretations shift and change over time, suggesting new challenges to old assumptions? My study is strictly historical, not exegetical (on my part). I have let the theologians speak for themselves. What I discovered, however, has confirmed my hypothesis. The traditional understanding of 1 Timothy 2:11–14 was authoritative because it was grounded in the creation ordinances. Consequently, it was applicable to *all* human society. In fact, the creation ordinances were of greater consequence in civil society and the state than in the church, as the church was animated by a new order in which God the Holy Spirit breaks through in ways that are sometimes *contra mundum*.

The focus of my research was the interpretations given to 1 Timothy 2:11–14 by prominent Protestant commentators, representing a wide variety of church traditions. I found that those theologians who wrote after the mid-nineteenth century and claimed to be traditionalists (or today's complementarians) actually broke substantially with the theologians who wrote before that time. The nineteenth century was a watershed period, even for those who claim theological continuity with the past. Consequently, after examining commentaries written before this time, I give an overview of the nineteenth-century women's rights movement. I concentrate on the early women's rights movement because of its close association with contemporary spiritual revivals and reform efforts in the English-speaking world.

The changes wrought during this tumultuous time clearly had a significant impact on the way theologians would interpret 1 Timothy 2 in subsequent centuries.

In summary, the first part of this monograph examines Bible commentaries written before the mid-nineteenth century; these commentaries form the basis of the authentic traditional understanding of 1 Timothy 2. In this section I also digress briefly into a discussion of how early Protestant communities understood the relationship between the kingdom of Christ and the kingdom of this world. The second section is an overview of the nineteenth-century women's rights movement, as mentioned above. Thirdly, I briefly survey more recent interpretations of 1 Timothy 2, especially those commentaries that claim to uphold a "traditional" exegesis of the passage. I close with some observations on my research and the implications my findings have for further studies.

Before listing the theologians chosen for this survey, I should explain why I have omitted verses 9–10 and verse 15, which are all of a piece with the verses that are the subject of my study. The initial part of this passage concerns modest attire and already has been "relativized." What is considered modest today is quite different from what was considered modest just sixty years ago, not to mention fifteen hundred years ago. The principle holds—but how? Although verses 9–10 were the primary focus of some of the earlier exegetes, this problem receives little attention in churches today. Tackling this issue is beyond the scope of my study. On the other hand, verse 15 has always been considered difficult, in that it implies a salvation by works (childbearing) not faith. All the Protestant exegetes in my study wrestle with that and come up with various solutions to the problem; but that, too, is beyond the scope of this study. I am focusing exclusively on historic interpretations of 1 Timothy 2:11–14 and how these interpretations relate to creation ordinances and the role of women in the church and society.

Although commentaries written from the Reformation through the early nineteenth century provide a baseline, more recent commentaries also play an important role in this study. The number of commentaries published in this later period grew significantly, and at the same time include notable changes in how 1 Timothy 2:11–14 is interpreted. Consequently, the commentaries selected from the late nineteenth, twentieth, and twenty-first centuries are designed primarily to illustrate these changes. Since there are so many commentaries from this later period, my sample represents a smaller percentage of what is available; however, I still tried to include a broad spectrum of denominational backgrounds. Also, in order to maintain continuity with earlier exegetes concerning assumptions about the authority of Scripture, the commentaries I use from this later period are primarily the work of conservative theologians.

In my selection of commentaries, I consulted with numerous contemporary theologians, church historians, and written resources to identify the most prominent and influential exegetes. This was especially important in identifying interpretations that prevailed prior to the nineteenth-century era of reform. Apart from Luther (1483–1546) and Calvin (1509–64), I confined my research to the English-speaking world. During the centuries immediately following the Reformation, there are fewer commentaries from which to choose, and consequently it is easier to identify prominent representatives of the various Protestant traditions. Focusing my efforts on those theologians who wrote commentaries on 1 Timothy further narrowed the field.

I start with Luther and Calvin. The findings here are the most instructive, in spite of—or perhaps because of—being the oldest. Following these two are Matthew Poole (1624–79) and Mathew Henry (1662–1714), both Puritan exegetes. Poole's exegesis is taken from his *Commentary on the Holy Bible*, a work he started but was completed by friends after his death. Henry's massive biblical commentary was released in installments between 1704 and 1714. Next I examine John Gill, an English Baptist and "high Calvinist," whose three-volume New Testament commentaries were published between 1746 and 1748. Following Gill is Anglican clergyman Thomas Scott, an evangelical, who issued his commentaries in installments from 1788 to 1792. From the Methodist tradition, I investigate the writings of Adam Clarke, ordained by John Wesley and the primary Methodist scholar of his time. His commentaries were released in England between 1810 and 1826. Lastly, I briefly mention Presbyterian theologian Charles Hodge (1797–1878) and Anglican Bishop Charles Ellicott (1816–1905), as they appear to be the last two prominent theologians taking something approximating the traditional view. My survey is not exhaustive, but does, I believe, uncover the distinguishing features of the true traditional interpretation of the 1 Timothy 2 passage. All of the above theologians are highly regarded scholars, and their commentaries were/are read extensively across the English-speaking world. They represent the best of what is available.

1

The Authentic Traditional Interpretation

MARTIN LUTHER begins his discussion of 1 Timothy 2:11 by connecting it to previous verses, in that "Paul is still speaking of public matters." He goes on to say, "I also want it to refer to the public ministry, which occurs in the public assembly of the church."[1] The clear implication here is that "public matters" is a reference to female conduct in the public realm in general, but Luther extends this prohibition to include the church. What Luther says next needs to be read in full:

> She is not to be the spokesman among the people. She should refrain from teaching, from praying in public. She has the command to speak at home. This passage makes a woman subject. It takes from her all public office and authority. On the other side is the passage in Acts (8:27) about Queen Candace. We read many such examples in sacred literature—that women have been very good at management: Huldah, Deborah, Jael, the wife of the Kenite, who killed Sisera (2 Kings 22:14; Judges 4:14, 17). Why, then, does Paul say here that he deprives them of the administration

---

1. Luther, "Lectures on 1 Timothy," 276.

> of the Word as well as work? You should solve the argument in this way. Here we properly take "woman" to mean "wife," as he reveals from his correlative phrase (v. 12) "to have authority over man," that is, over her husband. He calls the husband "man," so he calls the wife "woman." Where men and women have been joined together, there the men, not the women, ought to have authority. An exceptional example is the case where they are without husbands, like Huldah and Deborah who had no authority over husbands. Another lived in Abela (II Samuel 20:14–21). The evangelist Philip had four unmarried daughters, etc. (cf. Acts 21:9). He forbids teaching contrary to a man or to have the authority of a man. Where there is a man, no woman should teach or have authority. Where there is no man, Paul has allowed that they do this, because it happens by a man's command. He wants to save the order preserved by the world—that a man be the head of a woman, as 1 Corinthians 11:3 tells us.[2]

At the beginning of this passage, Luther underscores the universality of female subordination in both church and state. Women are subject and are not to rule. That is the order "preserved by the world." However, having stated the basic premise of the passage, he then acknowledges exceptions in the world and in the church. The first exception he names is Candace, Queen of Ethiopia, who held a position of civil authority. Since she is listed along with such women as Deborah and Huldah, women who held positions of spiritual authority, Luther, in naming exceptions, under-

2. Ibid., 276–77.

scores the universality, in both church and state, of the basic principle. However, it is clear he also struggled with reconciling God's work in history, as revealed in Scripture, with Paul's admonitions. Luther resolves this apparent inconsistency by taking the word *gynē* to mean "wife" and *anēr* to mean "husband." Therefore, the numerous exceptions listed above may be allowed if the rule of wives over husbands is avoided. Nevertheless, he goes on to build a case against women teaching or ruling over men in the general sense.

Luther then moves on to vs. 12. In English, his words are translated "to have authority." He explains that this means "she ought not take over for herself the heritage which belongs to a man so that a man says to her: 'My lord.' She wants her own wisdom to have priority, that whatever she has said should prevail and whatever the man says should not."[3] We must conclude then that Luther sees this verse as a prohibition against women flaunting their wisdom over that of a man. The same spirit would be captured in a prohibition against women domineering men or usurping authority that rightly belongs to men.

First Timothy 2:13 makes it clear that Paul is not speaking arbitrarily, but that his principles are derived from creation. Luther later summarizes this position in his discussion of verse 14, by saying, "God himself has so ordained that man be created first—first in time and first in authority. His first place is preserved in the Law."[4] Luther also argues from experience, which he believes has shown man to be superior in wisdom and courage. Finally, male headship is further reinforced by Eve's role in the fall. It was not Adam

3. Ibid., 277.
4. Ibid., 278.

who went astray. Satan successfully approached and deceived the weaker vessel. "Adam sinned knowingly, but he wanted to agree with his wife and please her."[5] Creation and the fall establish Adam as superior in rank and in constitution (wisdom and courage).

Luther then goes into a rather lengthy exposition of verse 15. He brings his entire discussion of verses 9–15 to a close with the following statement: "Thus you see how he wants Christian women to behave in public life, in the home, etc. If the Lord were to raise up a woman for us to listen to, we would allow her to rule like Huldah. This first part was spoken to husbands and wives. What follows is the description of other estates—of bishops and of deacons."[6] Although Luther's treatment of verses 9–15 is extensive and certainly digresses into general principles of male headship, he concludes by acknowledging the possibility of women within the Christian community exercising leadership under extraordinary circumstances and the primacy of the married relationship in understanding verses 11–12. Of special note are Luther's application of this passage to public life in general; his reference to the fact that male headship is the order "preserved by the world," as 1 Corinthians 11:3 tells us; and his additional comment, in the context of discussing creation, that this is the order "preserved by the Law."

No doubt John Calvin was familiar with Luther's commentaries. Calvin was considered the greatest exegete of his time and is still considered authoritative today. There is a remarkable coherence in his exegeses that creates complex connections between specific passages and the broader

---

5. Ibid.
6. Ibid., 280.

principles of the Christian faith. It seems as if one must know all of Calvin to truly understand any part of Calvin, yet I believe he has written enough on the subject at hand to put his ideas into their rightful context. By looking at the specific words he uses in his exegeses we can make correct assumptions about connections to his larger systematic worldview.

Calvin explains Paul's instructions in 1 Timothy 2:11 as bidding women "learn quietly; for quietness means silence, that they may not take upon them to speak in public."[7] Calvin then expands on Paul's argument in verse 12, which I think should be read in total:

> *But I suffer not a woman to teach.* Not that he takes from them the charge of instructing their family, but only excludes them from the office of teaching, which God has committed to men only. On this subject we have explained our views in the exposition of the First Epistle to the Corinthians. If anyone bring forward by way of objection, Deborah (Judges 4:4) and others of the same class, of whom we read that they were at one time appointed by the command of God to govern the people, the answer is easy. Extraordinary acts of God do not overturn the ordinary rules of government, by which he intended that we should be bound. Accordingly, if women at one time held the office of prophets and teachers, and that too when they were supernaturally called to it by the Spirit of God, He who is above all law might do this; but being a particular case, this is not opposed to the constant and ordinary system of government.

---

7. Calvin, *Commentaries on the Epistles to Timothy*, 67.

> He adds—what is closely allied with the office of teaching—*and not to assume authority over the man*; for the very reason, why they are forbidden to teach, is, that it is not permitted by their condition. They are subject, and to teach implies the rank of power or authority. Yet it may be thought that there is no great force in this argument; for even prophets and teachers are subject to kings and other magistrates. I reply, there is no absurdity in the same person commanding and likewise obeying, when viewed in different relations. But this does not apply to the case of woman, who by nature (that is, by the ordinary law of God) is formed to obey; for γυναικοκρατία (the government of women) has always been regarded by all wise persons as a monstrous thing; and therefore, so to speak, it will be a mingling of heaven and earth, if women usurp the right to teach. Accordingly, he bids them be "quiet," that is, keep within their own rank.[8]

For what reasons are women made subject? The argument is that it is so by God's command, as revealed in the order of creation. In addition, woman's condition is compounded and made "less agreeable" by Eve's role in the fall. However, Calvin refutes the notion that Adam fell into sin because he was overcome by the allurements of his wife and wanted to please her. Both Adam and Eve, says Calvin, were deceived by the wiles of the devil.[9] It also should be noted that although Calvin considers the rule of women to be a monstrous thing,[10] he never produces a litany of feminine

8. Ibid., 67–68.
9. Ibid., 69–70.
10. It should be noted that Calvin's commentary was published

qualities that make women unfit for leadership. This directive, that woman be subject, is grounded in the will of God, as decreed in the creation ordinances.

Now, what conclusions can we draw from all of the above? It is clear from the simple reading of the text that Calvin believes women are excluded from all public teaching and leadership in both church and state. This principle is grounded in "the ordinary rules of government" and "the true order of nature."[11] However, he also acknowledges, at least within the church, the possibility of cases *particulier et extraordinaire*.[12] The fact that God's commands at creation are binding on human society in its ordinary business does not mean that God cannot supersede the law of nature if he wills. In addition, it is not like Calvin to use language in a haphazard way. To understand what Calvin means by "the ordinary law of God" and "the true order of nature," we must further investigate his understanding of the relationship between the kingdom of Christ and the kingdom of this world.

Since the beginning of church history, theologians have struggled with how the kingdom of God should interact with the kingdom of this world. Augustine's *City of God*, written while the Roman Empire was literally falling down around him, was the first major work dedicated to this subject. Throughout the medieval period, scholars continued to develop theories articulating the appropriate realms of authority occupied by the two kingdoms. Closely aligned with

prior to John Knox's notorious *First Blast of the Trumpet Against the Monstrous Regimen of Women* (1558). I find it interesting that Knox chose to use the word "monstrous" in his title, which, in that age, is best understood as meaning "unnatural."

11. Calvin, *Commentaries on the Epistles to Timothy*, 68.
12. Ibid., 67 n2.

that was the study of natural law, reaching perhaps its most famous expression in the writings of Thomas Aquinas. In recent years, scholars have been re-discovering early Protestant understandings of natural law and the two kingdoms.[13]

Both Luther and Calvin wrote extensively on these issues, building on the work of their predecessors but also charting new ground. It is not my intention to delve into the particulars of the reformers' views on natural law and the two kingdoms, except as they shed light on interpretations of the 1 Timothy 2 passage. Luther and Calvin both defended the moral goodness of the sword-bearing state and Christians' participation in that state. They believed Christians were citizens of two kingdoms, both ordained by God. These two kingdoms, however, operate for different ends and under very different rules. The spiritual kingdom is expressed on earth in the church, which has a redemptive and eschatological purpose. It does not bear the sword and submits to the redemptive ethic of Scripture, as revealed in Jesus Christ. On the other hand, the temporal kingdom of this world can use the sword and is based in natural law. Natural law, for the reformers, is that law that is imprinted on the consciences of humankind (Rom 2:14–15) and found in the moral principles underlying the Mosaic law. Natural law also finds its origin in the creation ordinances. God rules both kingdoms. In the church or spiritual kingdom, he rules as redeemer in Jesus Christ; in the state and other social institutions, he rules as creator and sustainer.[14] Sin has marred human ability to

13. I draw much of my information on this subject from David VanDrunen's book *Natural Law and the Two Kingdoms, A Study in the Development of Reformed Social Thought*.

14. VanDrunen, *Natural Law and the Two Kingdoms*, 2, 56–57,

fully discern natural law outside of God's special revelation and regenerating grace; nevertheless, it is through the remnants of natural law that God graciously restrains the consequences of sin in this world.[15]

These ideas as developed by Luther and then Calvin had a formative impact on other Protestant traditions beyond the early Reformation. The difficulties arose in applying these principles to practical situations. The church existed in this world, and there were numerous areas in which the church and state or church and culture shared overlapping jurisdictions. Consequently, what was separated in theory might, in reality, have implications for both the spiritual and temporal realms.

Luther led in developing the Protestant understanding of natural law and the two kingdoms. God's spiritual kingdom is represented on earth by the church and operates under the redemptive ethic of Jesus Christ. The kingdom of this world and its representative institutions find their origin in natural law as described above. Although, according to VanDrunen, Luther never expressly connected natural law with eternal law (that law which governs God's kingdom as manifested in the church), he assigned the "external" government of the church to the care of the state.[16] So, in reality, the two kingdoms shared overlapping jurisdictions.

Fleshing out the relationship between the two kingdoms was not easy, and boundaries were sometimes

63–65, 71–72, 99–100. In some respects my work is a case study confirming VanDrunen's thesis.

15. Helm, "Calvin and Natural Law," 190.

16. VanDrunen, *Natural Law and the Two Kingdoms*, 58–59.

muddled. I would contend, however, that Luther placed the basis of the subordination of women to men in natural/creational law. Consequently, although he saw the subordination of women as operative in the church, it was an import, so to speak, from the temporal world. That is what Luther meant in his exegesis of 1 Timothy 2:11 and 1 Corinthians 11:3 when he says, "He [Paul] wants to save the order preserved by the world—that a man be the head of a woman." Again, when Luther is explaining 1 Timothy 2:13, he says, "His [Adam's] first place is preserved by the Law." This, too, is referring to the law of nature / creational law; the law that governs the kingdom of this world, or should govern this world if humankind is to prosper.

The fact that female subordination is not organic to the kingdom of Christ and His church is explained more fully in Luther's exegesis of Galatians 3:28: "In the world, and according to the sinful nature, there is a great difference and inequality of persons, and this must be observed carefully [. . .]. But in Christ there is no law, nor difference of persons, there is only one body, one spirit, one hope, one Gospel (Eph 4:4–6)."[17] Here again, when Luther uses the word "law," I believe he is referring to natural law. This law applies to the church in so far as the church should observe order and avoid confusion, but ultimately, according to Luther, the Christian conscience "knows nothing of the law—but has only Christ before its eyes."[18]

I don't believe Luther would refer to the subordination of women in the church as the law of the Gospel, as

---

17. Luther, "Lectures on Galatians," 356.
18. Ibid.

some later theologians do.[19] This kind of language would seem confusing to him and his understanding of the two kingdoms. It is also inconsistent with the dichotomy Luther builds between law and grace.[20] Female subordination is a principle observed in the church, but it finds its origin in the laws that define civil society, not the church. Calvin builds on Luther's understanding of natural law and the two kingdoms and makes more explicit application of this rubric to his treatment of 1 Timothy 2.

Calvin had a very high view of the state and its God-ordained function in temporal matters. Of his two-kingdoms theology he repeatedly says, "the spiritual kingdom of Christ and civil government are things very widely separated,"[21] yet they do not exist in opposition to one another. In fact, believers benefit from God's work of creation and preservation, the basis for civil society, and thus share a common work with non-believers. There is a twofold government of all humankind. The church addresses the spiritual and internal while civil institutions relate to "the external regulation of manners."[22] The relationship between men and women finds its basis in this external regulation of manners. (Neither Luther nor Calvin assign to the church the task of returning the world to its pristine state before the fall, based in creation ordinances.) The mission of the church is relatively narrow and specific

---

19. For example, see Hendriksen, *Exposition of the Pastoral Epistles*, 109.

20. See Appendix for a further explication of Luther's two-kingdoms view.

21. Calvin, *Institutes*, 4.20.1.

22. Ibid.

and rooted in the redemptive and eschatological work of Jesus Christ. According to VanDrunen, Calvin located the institutional manifestation of the spiritual kingdom in the church alone (not in the family, or any part of the society at large).[23] Natural law, on the other hand, forms the basis for the "regulation of manners" and civil and societal order in general.

However, when theory meets reality, the lines of demarcation are sometimes a bit fuzzy. Although Calvin repeatedly affirms the distinction between the spiritual authority of the church and the civil authority of the state, the two sometimes have an interest in one another and again share overlapping jurisdictions. In his instructions on civil government, Calvin assigns a rather expansive authority to the state when he says its task is to "foster and maintain the external worship of God, to defend sound doctrine and the condition of the Church, to adapt our conduct to human society, to form our manners to civil justice, to conciliate us to each other, to cherish common peace and tranquility."[24] Likewise, the affairs of the state sometimes impinge on the spiritual health of the church. In our lives together on this earth, the civil and spiritual will inevitably affect one another. For instance, the reformers took the rather radical step of removing marriage from the purview of the church and placing it under the authority of the state (further proof that they saw male/female relationships, and these based in creation ordinances, as temporal matters). In Calvin's Geneva, issues concerning marriage and the family were clearly under civil jurisdiction, yet the Consistory spent an inordinate amount

---

23. VanDrunen, *Natural Law and the Two Kingdoms*, 79.
24. Calvin, *Institutes*, 4.20.2.

of time addressing these issues, as they often had spiritual ramifications.[25] Decisions in domestic cases, however, were ultimately the responsibility of the state.

Calvin saw natural law (moral law, creation ordinances) as a universal standard for the development of civil law and ordained by God for such purposes. The principles that animate the church are egalitarian, as laid out in Galatians 3:28 and Colossians 3:11, and consequently one's "condition among men" (rank and privilege) is irrelevant in the spiritual realm.[26] Yet, as mentioned above, the civil order, including adapting our conduct to human society, is observed in the church.

In practical application, the appeals to natural law are not always precise. However, one thing Calvin makes abundantly clear is that natural law, grounded in Old Testament moral law, the creation order, and human conscience, can be adapted to differing historical circumstances without violating God's will. The specific judicial laws under Moses, for instance, are not necessarily an appropriate expression of natural law in other times and places. All civil law, says Calvin, should ultimately operate out of principles of equity and charity.[27]

In contrast, Christian liberty (not natural law) is foundational to life in the church. Calvin's writings on Christian liberty are extensive. Yet he repeatedly admonishes believers to use self-discipline and to behave with moderation. The principles of decency and order are the mediators of other lesser ordinances and traditions, within the life of the

25. VanDrunen, *Natural Law and the Two Kingdoms*, 87.
26. Calvin, *Institutes*, 4.20.1.
27. Ibid., 4.20.15; 4.20.16.

church. In book 4, chapter 10 of Calvin's *Institutes*, he elaborates on those lesser ordinances in some detail. As regards "decency," Calvin lists administering the sacraments with dignity, women appearing with heads covered in public, praying on one's knees, men worshipping with heads uncovered, and modes of burying the dead. Under "order," Calvin includes reverential behavior when the sermon is preached, the singing of hymns, days set apart for the celebration of the Lord's Supper, and Paul's prohibition against women teaching in the church.[28] All of these behaviors are of a kind and, in the church, take their direction from the broader principles of decency and order. When it comes to the role of women in the church, Calvin repeatedly appeals to decency and order, not the creation ordinances, further proof that he did not see creation ordinances as organic to the life of the church/spiritual kingdom. Later in book 4, chapter 10, Calvin sums up his position as follows:

> What? Is religion placed in a woman's bonnet, so that it is unlawful for her to go out with her head uncovered? Is her silence fixed by a decree which cannot be violated without the greatest wickedness? Is there any mystery in bending the knee, or burying a dead body, which cannot be omitted without a crime? By no means. For should woman require to make such haste in assisting a neighbour that she had not time to cover her head, she sins not in running out with her head uncovered. And there are some occasions on which it is not less seasonable for her to speak than on others to be silent. Nothing, moreover,

---

28. Calvin, *Institutes*, 4.10.29.

forbids him who, from disease, cannot bend his knees, to pray standing [. . .]. Nevertheless, in those matters the custom and institutions of the country, in short, humanity and the rules of modesty itself, declare what is to be done or avoided.[29]

In concluding this chapter, Calvin writes, "Lastly, instead of here laying down any perpetual law for ourselves, let us refer the whole end and use of observances to the edification of the Church, at whose request without offence allow not only something to be changed, but even observances which were formerly in use to be inverted."[30] This is indeed a provocative statement, given the fact that Calvin includes Paul's prohibitions against women teaching in the church in his list of "observances" that might be altered under varying circumstances.

Calvin's exegeses of the various Bible passages concerning women in the church are consistent with the above discourse. He wrestles with the sometimes seemingly inconsistent passages concerning the relationship between men and women and brings them all into a coherent whole in his understanding of the two kingdoms. For instance, Calvin recognizes that in 1 Corinthians 11:3 the man is placed in an intermediate position between Christ and the woman.[31] Yet, at the same time, in Galatians 3:28, Paul says "in Christ there is neither male nor female." Calvin resolves this di-

29. Calvin, *Institutes*, 4.10.31 See the Appendix for a more complete reading.

30. Ibid., 4.10.32.

31. Calvin, *Commentary on the Epistles to the Corinthians*, 353–54.

lemma as follows: "When he [Paul] says that there is no difference between the man and the woman, he is treating [*sic*] of Christ's spiritual kingdom, in which external qualities are not regarded or made any account of."[32] This spiritual kingdom has its present expression in the church, and, in fact, it is this Christian liberty and equality that underlie the Protestant doctrine of the priesthood of all believers. However, in this world our liberty and equality in Christ always should respect social order and decorum. Therefore, Calvin goes on to qualify his position: "In the meantime, however, he does not disturb civil order or honorary distinctions, which cannot be dispensed with in ordinary life. Here [in 1 Corinthians 11], on the other hand, he reasons respecting outward propriety and decorum—which is part of ecclesiastical polity."[33]

Calvin later again re-affirms this principle, shared with Luther, that male headship reflects "external arrangement and political decorum."[34] He would regard today's popular assignation to men of "spiritual headship" as a strange comingling of spiritual and temporal kingdom principles. In accordance with common Protestant doctrine, Calvin says that the spiritual head of the woman is Christ only; however, in the kingdom of this world she is subject to man. His exact words are as follows:

> Hence as regards spiritual connection in the sight of God, and inwardly in the conscience, Christ is the head of the man and of the woman without any distinction, because, as to that, there is no

32. Ibid., 354.
33. Ibid.
34. Ibid.

regard paid to male or female; but as regards external arrangement and political decorum, the man follows Christ and the woman the man, so that they are not upon the same footing, but, on the contrary, this inequality exists."[35]

In regards to 1 Corinthians 11 and 1 Timothy 2, I believe we can conclude that when Calvin speaks of "in ordinary life" or "the ordinary law of God," he is referring to the civil order. In 1 Timothy 2, Calvin also says women are made subject by "the true order of nature, which proceeded from the command of God."[36] I believe we can take that to be the natural law as expressed in creation ordinances, the basis for civil order. In his closing remarks on 1 Timothy 2:13, Calvin writes, "Since, therefore, God did not create two chiefs of equal power, but added to the man an inferior aid, the Apostle justly reminds us of that order of creation in which the eternal and inviolable appointment of God is strikingly displayed."[37] This language is noticeably similar to the language Calvin uses to describe natural law elsewhere.[38] Consequently, I believe Calvin sees male headship / female submission as a universal principle as it pertains to the governance of civil society. It may assume different expressions in different times and places, but the principle, as a foundation of the civil order, is absolute. This general understanding of the relationship between men and women in civil society, as dictated by the order of creation / natural law, is assumed implicitly or explicitly by all the exegetes

35. Ibid.
36. Calvin, *Commentaries on the Epistles to Timothy*, 68.
37. Ibid., 69.
38. Calvin, *Institutes*, 4.20.15.

examined in my study until the mid-nineteenth century. In addition, both Luther and Calvin placed the external government of the church under civil polity, which dictated the subordination of women to men in the church. I will make frequent references to natural law and the two kingdoms throughout this monograph, as I believe it is impossible to understand the authentic traditional interpretation of 1 Timothy 2:11–14 (and why it disappeared) outside of this framework.

Heirs to the Calvinist tradition, the Puritans were the first of the English-speaking exegetes to add their substantial insight to the 1 Timothy 2 passage. Among the early Puritan theologians, Matthew Poole has written the most helpful commentary. Like a number of other early commentators, Poole places most of his emphasis on verse 9. In fact, he devotes more space to his discussion of verse 9 than he does to his composite discussion of verses 11–14. Much of what he says about verses 11–14 reads more like a paraphrase. He does, however, elaborate in his discussion of verse 12, particularly in regards to women with an extraordinary call. His explanation reads as follows:

> *But I suffer not a women to teach;* not to teach in the public congregation, except she be a prophetess, endued with extraordinary gifts of the Spirit, as Mary, and Anna, and Huldah, and Deborah, and some women in the primitive church, concerning whom we read, I Cor. xi. 5, that they prophesied. *Nor to usurp authority over the man*: ordinary teaching of the woman was a usurpation of authority over the man, who is the head, which the apostle also forbade in I Cor. xi. 3, and here repeateth. It is probable that the speaking

> of some women in the church who had extraordinary revelations, imboldened others also to aim at the like, which the apostle here directs his speech against.[39]

Elsewhere in his discussion of passages dealing with women in the church, Poole repeatedly supports the legitimacy of women with an extraordinary call.[40]

However, in the context of his 1 Timothy exegesis it is impossible to determine whether or not Poole takes the traditional position concerning creation ordinances and the temporal kingdom. Consequently, we must search for clues elsewhere. In the above quote Poole references Paul's words in 1 Corinthians 11:3, concerning male headship. His comparison between the Christ/God and the woman/man relationships, as two persons equal in nature and essence but different in function, is similar to that of contemporary complementarian exegetes.[41] However, elsewhere Poole describes the headship of man over woman as being "political or economical."[42] Nowhere does Poole describe that headship as spiritual. In fact, in his initial discussion of 1 Corinthians 11:3, Poole argues that when Paul says that the "head of every man is Christ," he is referring to all church members, male and female, since Christ is the spiritual head of men and women alike.[43] So, I believe we can conclude that Poole holds to a two-kingdoms view and that the creation order and the fall place woman in a lower, inferior rank in

39. Matthew Poole, *A Commentary on the Holy Bible*, 778.
40. Ibid., 577, 591.
41. Ibid., 576.
42. Ibid., 577.
43. Ibid., 576.

the temporal (Poole's "political, economical") kingdom. However, in the spiritual kingdom, men and women are designed to be of mutual help to one another, being "equal in the Lord as to the state of grace, in Christ there is *neither male nor female* [. . .] when we come to consider them as to their spiritual state, and in their spiritual reference, there is no difference."[44] Under ordinary circumstances women are not to exercise leadership over men in the church; nevertheless, the principles of headship and submission are not organic to the spiritual kingdom / church.

Also a Puritan, Matthew Henry, like Poole, does not explicitly expound on a two-kingdoms theology. Yet, it is implied in both his exposition of 1 Timothy 2 and 1 Corinthians 14. Since Henry's treatment of 1 Corinthians 14 is considerably more detailed than 1 Timothy 2, I will focus my attention there.

Concerning the extraordinary call, Henry first presents an abbreviated version of the seeming contradiction—that in one place Paul recognizes that women pray and prophesy (prophesying meaning to teach) and at another point he admonishes women to be silent and not to teach. In Henry's resolution of the conflict, we hear echoes of Poole, Luther, and Calvin:

> Or, why should they have this gift, if it must never be publically exercised? For these reasons, some think that these general prohibitions are only to be understood in common cases; but on extraordinary occasions, when women were under a divine *afflatus*, and known to be so, they might have liberty of speech. They were not or-

---

44. Ibid., 578.

dinarily to teach, nor so much as to debate and ask questions in the church, but learn in silence there; and if difficulties occur, *ask their own husbands at home*.[45]

In the context of 1 Corinthians 14, Henry justifies Paul's instructions by saying they are commandments from God. Woman is made subordinate to man and should refrain from any behavior that might suggest she is trying to change ranks. Henry elaborates by saying that "speaking in public seemed to imply, at least at that age, and among that people" an indecent assumption of superiority on the part of a woman. The same would apply to public teaching. Consequently, such behavior would be shameful in the church as well.[46] The principle to be observed in civil society (and therefore, the church) was female subordination. The specific behaviors that were forbidden *at that time* were speaking and teaching in public assemblies. The temporal kingdom, reflecting God's created order, forbade women to engage in public speaking and teaching. It would be most indecent for the church to do otherwise. Henry's language is similar to Calvin's, so we assume he had similar understandings concerning the position of women in the temporal kingdom.

The Puritans wrote prolifically on many subjects. In their ordinary tracts, treatises, and sermons, we find a great deal on family relationships. William Gouge wrote a 700-page tome on family life, entitled *Of Domesticall Duties* (1622). The role of women in the church was not the focus of

45. Matthew Henry, *An Exposition of the Old and New Testaments*, 583.

46. Ibid.

his exertions; however, he makes reference to 1 Timothy 2. Gouge agrees that women have liberty to teach in their own homes, and what is forbidden in 1 Timothy 2:12 is public teaching; "that branch of teaching hath respect to publike assemblies, and Churches, in which she may not teach."[47] This again confirms the understanding that women were forbidden to teach and usurp authority over men in the public arena in general, which included church gatherings.

Puritans believed that God governed the civil kingdom through a series of hierarchical relationships, which included the authority of husbands over wives and by implication, men over women.[48] Ironically, however, they also developed Calvin's social/political thought in some interesting directions, which eventually undermined the staying power of hierarchies. They spoke of binding relationships as covenants. Thus, they referred to the basis of civil authority (the kingdom of this world) as the covenant of works and the basis of the spiritual kingdom as the covenant of grace. Marriage also was a covenant relationship. I will follow this trajectory back from the nineteenth century when we look at the women's rights movement.

The next exegete, John Gill, was a Baptist and a Calvinist. In his discussion of verse 11, he says women should not be teachers but learners, and they should do so in silence. Any questions they have, they should ask their husbands at home (where they have permission to teach, in their families). In public worship, they are not to "rise and speak, under a pretence of having a word from the Lord, or being under the impulse of the Spirit of the Lord,

---

47. William Gouge, *Of Domesticall Duties*, 258.
48. Edmund Morgan, *Puritan Family*, 18–19.

as some frantic women have done."[49] Since the First Great Awakening was at its height when Gill's commentaries were published (1746–48), that may be an oblique reference to female participation in the fervor of revival. (Gill was a close associate of George Whitfield.) Regarding verse 12, Gill writes that the woman is not to:

> usurp authority over the man; as not in civil and political things, or in things relating to civil government; and in things domestic, or the affairs of the family; so not in things ecclesiastical, or what relate to the church and government of it; for one part of rule is to feed the church with knowledge and understanding; and for a woman to take upon her to do this, is to usurp authority over the man.[50]

I take Gill's logic at face value here—if not in the civil realm, so then not in the church. According to verse 13, woman is subordinate to man because she was "made out of him and for him." And this proves, according to Gill, "that the woman's subjection to man is according to the laws of nature and creation."[51] Gill believes that verse 14 teaches that Eve was truly deceived while Adam was not. Similar to Luther, he says that Adam ate the forbidden fruit out of love for his wife, "from a fond affection to her, to bear her company, and that she might not die alone."[52]

In conclusion, Gill appears to have an understanding of natural law and the two kingdoms that characterized

49. John Gill, *Exposition of the New Testament*, 599.
50. Ibid., 600.
51. Ibid.
52. Ibid.

most of the reformers up to this point. The subordination of women is grounded in natural law/creation ordinances. Therefore, as women are not to usurp authority over men in the civil realm, so they are not to do so in the ecclesiastical. Unlike the other theologians cited, Gill makes no accommodation for an extraordinary call among women. The silence imposed on them appears to be absolute. This seems a bit ironic, given the record of the Baptists during the Second Great Awakening in America. However, we now turn our attention to the great evangelical revival in England.

Ordained an Anglican priest some years earlier, Thomas Scott became a Christian during this period of revival through his association with John Newton. Scott's widely read commentary series came out between 1788 and 1792. Like Matthew Poole he devotes most of his attention in the 1 Timothy 2 passage to verse 9; that is, to issues concerning women's apparel. His treatment of verses 11–14 reads much like a paraphrase. However, also like Poole, he remarks on exceptions to Paul's rule as it is laid down in verse 12: "This rule admitted of an exception, in the case of those, who spoke by the Spirit of prophesy."[53] He again refers to women under "an extraordinary impulse of the Holy Spirit" in his exegesis of 1 Corinthians 14.[54] In the church the Holy Spirit can and will do things that are sometimes *contra mundum*.

His views on creation ordinances and the temporal kingdom are implied in his brief discussion of 1 Timothy 2:14, where he says "women [. . .] ought not to affect author-

53. Thomas Scott, *Holy Bible*, 428.
54. Ibid., 187.

ity, or presume to be public teachers."[55] The application here seems to be to the public sphere in general. Furthermore, in his interpretation of 1 Corinthians 11:2–16, Scott remarks that man is the *image and glory of God* in his (man's) appointment as God's representative "in ruling over this lower world." It is in this lower world that the woman is subordinate to the man, she being "the most honorable subject of his delegated authority."[56] Nowhere does Scott refer to the man as her spiritual head. So here again, we have evidence of a two-kingdoms paradigm, with woman being made subordinate to man in the civil kingdom. Closely associated with the evangelical revival in England was the rise of Methodism.

Wesley (1703–1791) did not write an extensive commentary on either the 1 Timothy or 1 Corinthian passages concerning the role of women in the church. In his *Notes* on 1 Timothy 2, he remarks that woman was originally the "inferior," and per Paul's instructions in 1 Corinthians 14, he writes: "Let your women be silent in the churches—Unless they are under extraordinary impulse of the Spirit. For in other cases it is not permitted for them to speak—by way of teaching in public assemblies. But to be in subjection—To the man whose proper office it is to lead and to instruct the congregation."[57]

However, Wesley's brevity is more than compensated for by the extensive exegesis of Methodist theologian Adam Clarke. Consequently, I will focus my attention on Clarke. Although Clarke's development of a two-kingdoms theology

55. Ibid., 429.
56. Ibid., 168.
57. John Wesley, *Explanatory Notes*.

is not as explicit as in Luther or Calvin, it is clearly assumed in the remarks he makes on 1 Timothy 2 concerning God's design of man and woman and their roles in the temporal world. In fact, he quotes several Greek and Roman sources that testify to the rightness of God's created order as it applies to the kingdoms of this world.[58]

In treating 1 Timothy 2:11–12, Clarke defers to his earlier comments on 1 Corinthians 14:34–35, which I will do also. He believes it is evident in 1 Corinthians 11 that women did "prophesy or teach."[59] So, he, too, attempts to reconcile Paul's admonitions to silence with the biblical record. Clarke's attention to historical context adds an interesting dimension to the traditional exegesis of this passage. He discusses the low view of women espoused by certain rabbinic traditions, a view that persisted until the time of the gospel and the fulfillment of Joel's prophesy that the spirit of God would be poured out on women as well as men. He then reconciles the seeming inconsistency between the biblical record and Paul's instructions in 1 Corinthians (and 1 Timothy):

> Both places seem perfectly consistent. It is evident from the context that the apostle refers here to asking questions, and what we call dictating in the assemblies. It was permitted to any man to ask questions, to object, altercate, attempt to refute, etc., in the synagogue; but this liberty was not allowed to any woman. St. Paul confirms this in reference also to the Christian Church; he orders them to keep silence; and if they wish to learn

---

58. Adam Clarke, *New Testament of Our Lord and Savior Jesus Christ*, 593.

59. Ibid., 278–79.

anything, let them inquire of their husbands at home; for it is perfectly indecorous for women to be contending with men in public assemblies, on points of doctrine, cases of conscience, etc. But this by no means intimated that when a woman received any particular influence from God to enable her to teach, that she was not to obey that influence; on the contrary, she was to obey it, and the apostle lays down directions in chap. XI for regulating her personal appearance when thus employed.[60]

What Clarke believes is at issue in both 1 Corinthians and 1 Timothy is a spirit of contention and arrogance on the part of some women, evident in attempts to usurp the man's rightful authority. That is an authority grounded in creation, when God designed the man to be pre-eminent (and gave to women a "natural inferiority"). As a consequence of God's created order and Eve's role in the fall, God has subjected women to the government of man.[61] That is the order observed in the kingdom of this world, and Paul has in mind guarding the church against accusations of disorderly conduct. Paul is not attempting to suppress women who are acting in obedience to the Holy Spirit. Clarke takes the traditional position concerning the relationship between men and women in civil society, based on creation ordinances. However, in the church, under subjection to the Holy Spirit, he sees the possibility of a different order at work. Clarke, writing at the beginning of the nineteenth century, is the last of the major, traditional exegetes.

60. Ibid., 279.
61. Ibid., 593.

So, what are the salient points and principles that characterize the traditional exegesis of 1 Timothy 2:11–14? All the traditional theologians agree that the subordination of woman to man is grounded in creation ordinances and the fall. They also all recognize the creation ordinances as prescriptive in their application to civil order and civil society. There is a two-kingdom ideology explicit in Luther and Calvin and implicit in Poole, Henry, Gill, Scott, and Clarke. In addition, none of these exegetes see creation ordinances as organic to the kingdom of Christ and his church. However, the general strictures placed on women in society at large, derived from the creation order and Eve's role in the fall, also are observed in the church. There are two reasons given: (1) so that the church might not cause offense and be accused of disreputable conduct, and/or (2) because the church honors "the order preserved by the world," as Luther expressed it.

In addition, all the traditional exegetes seem comfortable with the word "usurp," as used in verse 12 in the King James Version of the Bible. This word rightly conveys their understanding of any attempt on the part of a woman to wrongly wrest rank and authority away from the man. They also use the word "inferior" without apology to describe the woman in relationship to the man. Again, this is because the traditional theologians see the creation ordinances as mandating the subordination of women to men in the temporal kingdom of this world, where social rank and inequality are ordinarily observed. Egalitarian principles govern the spiritual kingdom. Consequently, none of the traditional theologians assign to men a *spiritual* headship. In fact, Calvin, for one, explicitly rejects this idea. Male headship is important to the right functioning of civil society, finding its origin in God's creation ordinances, not in the redemptive and eschatological purposes of the church. (It should be noted that although boundaries between the spiritual and temporal kingdoms are not always clear, the spiritual kingdom is never equated solely with the next world. It is manifested in the life of the church on earth.)

In the church, here and now, there is the possibility of something *contra mundum*. All the traditional theologians, except John Gill, acknowledge the possibility of a woman with an extraordinary call. How that would operate practically in the life of the church is not addressed. Poole and Clarke seem least reluctant to recognize the extraordinary call, and Clarke even reprimands women who fail to act under the prompting of the Holy Spirit.

If the linchpin of the traditional exegesis is the intrinsic connection between the creation order and an orderly civil society, then we should attempt to follow this trail until it ends. The last two theologians in my survey who demonstrate this understanding are Charles Hodge and Charles Ellicott. Both depart from the traditionalists in some ways, but not in their application of creation ordinances to the culture at large.

In his commentary on 1 Corinthians, published in 1857, Hodge remarks, "It is not permitted for them [women] to speak [. . .]. The speaking intended is public speaking, and especially in the church."[62] Note that although he puts the emphasis on speaking in the church, he does include public speaking in general. However, elsewhere Hodge does

---

62. Charles Hodge, *Exposition of the First Epistle to the Corinthians*, 305.

not demonstrate an understanding of the traditional two-kingdoms logic. Earlier in his treatment of 1 Corinthians 14, he writes that since the early church did not permit women to speak publically, the practice must be considered "unchristian."[63] (I take this to mean that he sees the silence of women as organic to the spiritual kingdom / church.)

Finally, Ellicott, who published his commentary on 1 Timothy in the 1860s, makes the following comment in regards to verse 12: "Every form of public address or teaching is clearly forbidden as at variance with woman's proper duties and destination."[64] This is confirmed by the order of creation and Eve's role in the fall. *Ellicott's Commentary on the Whole Bible*, which appeared between 1877 and 1882, reiterates the above interpretation.[65] This was the last example I found of an exegetical position that clearly applies male headship / female subordination to the civil realm.

In conclusion, the traditional theologians see the creation ordinances as foundational to civil society and civil authority. The church, in turn, honors the order preserved by the world. But, what happens when the world is turned upside down?

---

63. Ibid., 304.

64. Charles John Ellicott, *Critical and Grammatical Commentary on the Pastoral Epistles*, 52.

65. Charles John Ellicott, ed., *Ellicott's Commentary on the Whole Bible*.

2

The Nineteenth Century: "A Mingling of Heaven and Earth"

IN HIS exegesis of 1 Timothy 2, Calvin describes placing women in positions of authority as a "mingling of heaven and earth." Ironically, there is no epithet that better describes the early nineteenth century in the English-speaking world. Before looking at events in the nineteenth century, I should mention that many books have been written on the topics I will discuss. The material is vast, and I must, of necessity, abbreviate and generalize. There are numerous books listed in the bibliography for those who wish to explore specific topics in more depth.

At the dawn of the nineteenth century, the status of woman in the English-speaking world was defined largely by her relationship to the family. She was subordinate to her husband; yet, ensconced in her separate domestic sphere, she was considered the "heart" of the home. In the popular mind, she was not only considered more delicate and sensitive than man, but also morally superior to him.[1] She also

---

1. For a popular rendition of female attributes see Sarah Stickney Ellis, *The Women of England, Their Social Duties and Domestic Habits* (London: Fisher and Son, 1839); also, Mrs. William Parkes, *Domestic Duties* (London: Longman, Hurst, Rees, Orme, Brown, and Green,

was considered better equipped than he to train and nurture children. Outside the domestic sphere, however, patriarchal norms still held sway and her identity was merged with that of her husband (or her father, if she was unmarried). According to English jurist William Blackstone, this doctrine of coverture meant that the husband and wife were one in the eyes of the law and that "one" was the husband.[2] Coverture, a principle that many considered to be not only grounded in tradition but also in scriptural principles concerning the husband/wife relationship (established at creation), had legal and social ramifications. The husband, for instance, was the wife's spokesman and representative in all public affairs outside the home. When a woman married, all her material goods became the property of her husband. He was ultimately responsible for any debts she might incur. If there was a divorce, the father was automatically awarded custody of the children. In addition, a woman's educational opportunities were severely restricted. It was thought that even brilliant young women, were they exposed to the academic rigors pursued by men on the university level, would be subject to physical breakdown and even death.[3] Furthermore, women were not allowed to participate in the political culture; again, it was presumed that their husbands or fathers represented their best interests and that it was

1825); also Isabella Beeton, *The Book of Household Management* (London: S. O. Beeton, 1861). My remarks must be general, so I am focusing primarily on the middle class. The circumstances and expectations among the very wealthy and the very poor were different.

2. Macfarlane, *Marriage and Love in England*, 287.
3. Degler, *At Odds*, 311–12.

inappropriate for women to compete with men in the rough and tumble of politics and business.

Women in the English-speaking world, however, were considerably better off than most women in other parts of the world. The impact of Christianity already had softened their lot. Polygamy, for instance, was considered an anathema in the West. The companionate marriage, an historical anomaly, was well established in the English-speaking world by the nineteenth century. Nevertheless, cultural norms were rooted in patriarchal assumptions. The restrictions placed on women in the Greco-Roman world, like those mentioned in the commentaries written by Henry and Clarke, had passed into law and tradition in the West. My previous section hopefully gave the reader an insight into Christianity's affirmation of culture in this regard.

Jesus did not directly challenge the social and political order of his day. Misogyny, like slavery, had been around since the beginning of time. Jesus did, however, indirectly undermine these two institutions, but only through the application of the principles of his kingdom (which he said was "not of this world") to the kingdoms of this world. Was that what he intended? His followers took a variety of tacks. Early church thought on celibacy, for instance, tended to reinforce misogynistic assumptions.[4] Other counter-cultural forces, however, also were at work.

When standing at the cusp of the nineteenth-century women's rights movement, there are two trajectories one can follow back through time to its roots. The more circuitous route runs back through the Enlightenment to seventeenth-century and late sixteenth-century Puritan social

4. Irwin, *Womanhood in Radical Protestantism*, 1–3.

and political thought. The more direct and obvious route runs back through the Second and First Great Awakenings, finding its roots in evangelical Protestantism. Both converge in the Protestant doctrine of the priesthood of all believers. I will deal with the first route as briefly as possible, with the understanding that I am condensing and generalizing in order not to get bogged down in a complex history of political thought.

John Locke wrote his *Second Treatise of Civil Government* (1690) largely as theoretical justification for the Glorious Revolution (1688). The principles he sets forth in this essay also formed the basis of the *Declaration of Independence* (1776). The theory of natural rights—that "all men are created equal and endowed by their Creator with certain inalienable rights . . ." would find its widest application in the robust individualism of early nineteenth-century America, a phenomena that was inextricably bound with the popular religious movements of that time. Among other things, these religious movements rejected rank and privilege and looked energetically to a millennial age of equality and justice.[5] Even women found their own voices and framed their own opinions on freedom and equality.

The ideas that were foundational to the liberal democracies of the nineteenth century are usually attributed to Locke and other prominent eighteenth-century Enlightenment philosophers. However, the principles of natural rights, the sovereignty of the people, social contract, freedom of conscience, and the right to revolution can all be found in the social and political thought of the seventeenth-

---

5. Hatch, "Democratization of Christianity and Character of American Politics," 97.

century Puritans. The most succinct example is found in chapter ninety-two of Roger William's *The Bloody Tenent of Persecution*, published in 1644. Here all the above principles are alluded to in one paragraph![6] After a lengthy discussion of Enlightenment thought, present-day historian Jacques Barzun makes the following summary statement:

> The outcome of what has been reviewed here—late 17th century critical thought, the events of 1688, and the writings of Locke, Voltaire, and Montesquieu—may be summed up in a few points: [. . .] the political ideas of the Puritans aiming at equality and democracy were now in the mainstream of thought, minus the religious component.[7]

Although I have emphasized the continuities between the seventeenth (Puritans) and eighteenth (Enlightenment) centuries, there were many discontinuities as well. Rationalism replaced biblical revelation as the basis of the above principles, for one. Nevertheless, it is doubtful that there ever would have been an American Revolution without Christianity, particularly in its Protestant form.[8] So, if the argument is made that the emancipation of women in the nineteenth century drew its inspiration from the spirit of 1776, we still are drawn back to the socio-political ramifications of early Protestant thought. Likewise, the nineteenth-century companionate marriage was also a product of early Protestantism.

---

6. Williams, "Bloody Tenent of Persecution," 243.
7. Barzun, *From Dawn to Decadence*, 364–65.
8. For a full treatment see Novak, *On Two Wings*.

The reformers transformed marriage from an institution that often was considered a necessary evil into one seen as a positive good. Although they eliminated marriage as a sacrament, the reformers created, by precept and example, a new kind of human relationship, one based on mutual consent and love. In the English-speaking world we again are drawn to the Puritans as the originators of the companionate marriage. (Not that such marriages did not exist before this time. Among the Puritans, however, the companionate marriage appears to have been the rule rather than the exception.) Although the wife was clearly subordinate to the husband, Puritan individualism had an impact on the wife's status. Spiritually, according to the doctrine of the priesthood of all believers, she was equal in her title to grace and equal in her responsibility to God.[9] Historian Edmund Morgan describes the Puritan wife as follows:

> The Puritan wife of New England occupied a relatively enviable position by comparison, say, with the wife of early Rome or the Middle Ages or even of contemporary England; for her husband's authority was strictly limited. He could not lawfully strike her, nor could he command her anything contrary to the laws of God, laws that were explicitly defined in the civil codes. In one respect she was almost his equal, for she had a "joint interest in governing the rest of their Family."[10]

By the nineteenth century, the woman's position in the home would be, for all practical purposes, one of "separate

9. Haller, *Rise of Puritanism*, 121.
10. Morgan, *Puritan Family*, 45.

but equal" status. The individual responsibility she had before God coupled with the interest she had in governing the family would become her conduit to greater participation in the world outside the home.

In addition, we can conclude from Puritan diaries that a remarkable number of Puritan marriages were true romances.[11] The degree of mutuality is impressive. Although parental advice did not go unheeded, we also find that "for the first time in history young men chose their brides and brides their husbands."[12] However, it should be noted that for the Puritans love was not romantic passion but a rational choice. Yes, they were allowed to choose the objects of their love but were then under obligation to live out that love in the vicissitudes of everyday life. Puritan love was not so much a cause of marriage as a product.[13] Marriage was a covenant relationship before God, entered into contractually with obligations incumbent on both parties.

Just as the Puritans advanced the right to revolution when the government did not meet its fundamental obligations to the governed, so they also allowed for divorce when the basic obligations of marriage were not met—in New England. (In England divorce law did not apply equally to husbands and wives until well into the nineteenth century.) A study of divorces granted in New England in the early seventeenth century finds the grounds of divorce to have been adultery, desertion, absences of a length of time (as determined by civil authorities), and in Connecticut, "fraudulent contract" and failure of the husband to provide

11. Smith, *Daughters of the Promised Land*, 42.
12. Ibid., 41.
13. Morgan, *Puritan Family*, 54.

for his wife.[14] The injured party was allowed to remarry. I have gone into detail on the roots of the companionate marriage because of the importance marriage and the family played in the lives of nineteenth-century women.

Developments in the eighteenth century added new dynamics to the companionate marriage. Personal choice and romantic attachment replaced religious motivations. The loss of community supports and constraints on marriage did not always work to the advantage of women;[15] even so, the important position they occupied in the home, coupled with religious revival, would afford nineteenth-century women new and unprecedented opportunities.

The second trajectory backward from the nineteenth century to the roots of the women's rights movement traverses some of the same territory as the first—and originates at essentially the same place. It, however, follows the spiritual center of Protestantism, not its socio-political implications. It is my contention that Protestant spiritual passion so ignited the ordinary people of the English-speaking world, repeatedly, from the seventeenth through the nineteenth centuries, that the populace in general was transformed. The language and values of the kingdom of God were so thoroughly assimilated into the culture at the grassroots level, that even non-believers were shaped by them and responded to appeals couched in spiritual kingdom (egalitarian) language. Consequently, those overlapping jurisdictions between the church / spiritual kingdom and the kingdom of this world expanded with the spiritual claiming an ever greater domain. This process began in England in

14. Ibid., 36–37.
15. Smith, *Daughters of the Promised Land*, 62–63.

the late sixteenth century with the rise of Puritanism and continued through most of the seventeenth century, was re-ignited by the First Great Awakening and Wesleyan revivals in the mid-eighteenth century, and culminated in the evangelical revivals and Second Great Awakening of the early nineteenth century. I will begin in England but then focus most of my attention on the United States, where movements of the Spirit were given wider range and were less inhibited by tradition.

After the death of Elizabeth I and the ascension to the throne of the Stuart line, the Puritan efforts to reform the English church were completely blocked. Consequently, they turned to publishing and preaching and in doing so, over time, transformed the whole of English society. As preachers, the Puritans were locked out of the established church, and therefore, were supported by ordinary people, as supplicant preachers and lecturers. Although they soon became the professional intellectual class, opposing traditional authority, custom, and vested interest, their primary concerns were always spiritual.[16] Puritan preaching stressed a constant call to repentance for the unsaved, the individual responsibility of the saved, and the ability of the individual through the guidance of the Holy Spirit to read and understand the Bible. External religious formalities were of little value next to the movement of the soul towards greater godliness. Puritan minister Richard Baxter expressed this internal focus as follows: "Pride, in fact, is a greater sin than drunkenness or whoredom; and humility is as necessary as sobriety and chastity."[17]

16. Haller, *Rise of Puritanism*, 5, 40, 53, 83, 145.
17. Baxter, *Reformed Pastor*, 145.

Their emphasis on individual conscience and moral responsibility gave women equal access with men to the life of the spirit. Of course, the individualism fostered by Puritanism created centrifugal tendencies within the movement, as it did in Protestantism in general. In the end, whether Presbyterian, independent, separatist, Baptist, Brownist, or Quaker, the passion of their faith and force of character would permeate English society, and it would never be the same. Puritan historian William Haller points out that the Puritan legacy in literature alone (Bunyan, Defoe, Milton) had a shaping influence on English life for generations.[18] The individualism implicit in Puritanism also had a democratizing effect. A spiritually energized national character and vocabulary were emerging, and would spread and be re-enforced by events in the eighteenth and nineteenth centuries.

I would like to digress slightly and take a closer look at the Society of Friends, or Quakers, a group to which Haller refers as the left wing of the Puritan movement.[19] In the nineteenth century, Quaker influence in reform movements (abolitionism, women's rights) would far outweigh their numbers. This is significant. Although they took a more expansive view than Luther or Calvin on the claims of the spiritual kingdom on the individual conscience, they appear to have held to a two-kingdoms understanding of church and state.[20] Among the Quakers, however, ecclesiastical organization was clearly a function of the spiritual

18. Haller, *Rise of Puritanism*, 21.

19. Ibid., 178.

20. See Barclay, *Apology for the True Christian Divinity*. Note the first section in "The Fourteenth Proposition."

kingdom, not civil polity, and was consequently very egalitarian, in accordance with their understanding of the gifts and callings of Christ's kingdom. Therefore, women had nearly the same opportunities as men to exercise spiritual leadership. However, when it came to leadership in the world outside the church, Quakers adhered to traditional understandings. William Penn's colony, for instance, did not give women equal rights or opportunities with men to participate in civil government. Contemporary views on creation ordinances prevailed in the temporal kingdom.

Other "fringe groups" in the Puritan movement, such as the Levellers, also followed the egalitarian principles in Protestantism to their logical conclusion. However, their ideas, when not bound by a two-kingdoms ideology, spilled over into politics. Although most of their democratic ideas would be mainstream one hundred years later, they were rejected as too radical in the seventeenth century. Consequently, these groups blazed brightly and then disappeared altogether. The Quakers, on the other hand, were certainly persecuted for their theological idiosyncrasies, but continued to grow and be influential. They did not suffer the fate of the Levellers because theirs was a spiritual kingdom. The general populace might find fault with the extent to which Quakers pressed their spiritual kingdom values, but the roots of their egalitarian order were understood and tolerated within their religious sect. These same spiritual values would make a frontal assault on the world outside the church during the eighteenth-century Great Awakening.

Like Puritanism, the Great Awakening (and Wesleyan revival in England) promoted a more active, individualistic form of Protestantism. Personal initiative was encouraged, not only in responding to the call to faith, but also in organizing prayer meetings, Bible studies, and exhorting one another to godliness. The revivals of this period sprang up in different places spontaneously, within no uniting framework except for the work of the Holy Spirit. While the theology of the Wesleyan revival in England was more Arminian, Calvinism dominated in the American revivals of this period. The leader of the Great Awakening in New England was Jonathan Edwards, who strove to balance intellect and emotion in winning the "affections" of the people to Christ. Edwards and the "New Lights" stressed the salvation of the individual soul—repentance, justification, and sanctification. In the South, evangelical Calvinism provided an alternative to the Church of England, and also fostered a more emotional and personal faith. Sometimes met with violent hostility by established church adherents, the Baptist farmer-preachers in the South later would plant Baptist churches throughout the West.[21] The Great Awakening challenged the old elites, ignored denominational differences, and was the first event in American history to defy the chasm between black and white.

The most widely recognized personality in the American colonies at this time was George Whitfield, the leading evangelist in the Great Awakening, making the Great Awakening the first truly national event in the life of the colonies. The evangelicals who emerged from these revivals not only sought to re-make their churches (usually along more egalitarian lines), but also to birth a new, Christian, nation. The boundaries separating the proper

21. Noll, *History of Christianity*, 98–101.

jurisdiction of church from state were collapsing, as the people became immersed in spiritual kingdom language and aspirations.

The Second Great Awakening (late eighteenth/early nineteenth centuries) had an even greater impact on American society, largely because of the many reform movements it spawned. Like the First Great Awakening, it was part of a worldwide Gospel movement. However, my focus will be primarily on the United States. Again, revival broke out spontaneously in different regions, fostering a more personal and "enthusiastic" faith among converts. The Baptist and Methodist churches grew dramatically, with itinerant preachers taking the lead in bringing the gospel to remote communities on the frontier. Charisma was more important than education, and again the divisions of class, race, and gender seemed to melt away while the flames of revival blazed. Preachers were intent on telling everyone who would listen what s/he had to do to be saved. The priesthood of all believers, as well as the conviction that all were equal in sin and salvation and moral responsibility, unleashed a new commitment to the Christian vision of "Your kingdom come, Your will be done on earth as it is in heaven." (Matt 6:10, NASB). Kingdom language and values were injected into every dark corner of society where sin and oppression kept the benighted in bondage. Prisons, asylums, sailors at sea, prostitutes, hospitals, taverns, schools, pagan nations—nothing and no one was beyond the reach of the gospel and the zeal of the reformers. The abolition of slavery was perhaps the most momentous of the reform movements, followed by the advance of the women's rights movement.

For many evangelicals and those who had ingested their spiritual kingdom language and values, it seemed as if the world was standing on the precipice of a heavenly vision, in which "The kingdom of the world has become the kingdom of our Lord and of His Christ . . ." (Rev 11:15, NASB). The principles of the Protestant Reformation were doing battle with what Luther had called "the great difference and inequality of persons" that existed in the kingdom of this world. The former would triumph over the latter, and for women this meant that Galatians 3:28 / the egalitarian principles of the spiritual kingdom would have the last word. Theology shaped history. Historian Nathan Hatch refers to this nineteenth-century awakening as "the very incarnation of the church into popular culture."[22]

I have not addressed the role of specific women during the revivals because I want to emphasize the grassroots "Christianization" of the society in general. That is fundamental to understanding the emancipation of women in the English-speaking world. Natural law / creation ordinances made women forever subordinate, but before the throne of grace, women were equally sinners, equally saved, and equally responsible. So, it should come as no surprise that there were female preachers long before there were elected female politicians, female evangelists long before there were female academicians. During the fervor of revival, women came forward claiming an extraordinary call, whether as teachers, evangelists, preachers, or exhorters. They publicly testified to what God had done in their lives and, like some of their male counterparts, were criticized and ostracized, but

22. Hatch, "Democratization of Christianity and Character of American Politics," 95.

rarely stopped. Women evangelists, of course, came under greater fire than men. Maria Stewart, an African Methodist, responded in a typical fashion: "What if I am a woman? Is not the God of ancient times the God of these modern days? Did He not raise up Deborah, to be a mother, and a judge in Israel? Did not Queen Esther save the lives of the Jews? And Mary Magdalene first declare the resurrection of Christ from the dead?"[23] In 1827, Harriet Livermore preached before the U.S. Congress, long before that august body would countenance a woman sitting among their ranks.[24] As the spiritual kingdom enlarged its claims on the civil kingdom, so women enlarged their sphere of influence.

The fact that female leadership and public speaking ran into less opposition in the context of religious revival than in the context of civic debate has traditionally been explained by feminist social historians as a function of power. Women exercising power in the political realm were more threatening to male hegemony than women exercising power in the religious realm. That, of course, reflects twentieth-century perspectives on the marginalization of religion. I contend, however, that in the early nineteenth century, religion was a much more powerful arbitrator of disputes within community life in the English-speaking world (especially the United States) than were political institutions.[25] Consequently, the exercise of "power" within religious communities is a significant topic of study for social historians. In addition, popular teachings concerning

23. Brekus, *Strangers and Pilgrims*, 280.

24. Ibid., 1.

25. For a full discussion see Hatch, "Democratization of Christianity and Character of American Politics," 96–97.

the biblical underpinnings for civil order, on the one hand, and concerning spiritual kingdom values, on the other, may have been extremely influential in shaping institutions and individual behavior. I believe we can assume that the teachings of the traditional Bible commentators concerning creation ordinances, the civil and spiritual kingdoms, and the roles of women in state and church actually had a formative impact on the thinking and actions of ordinary men and women. For instance, the fact that women had more visible roles in some churches long before they acquired leadership roles in the culture at large reflected traditional biblical teaching on the principles underlying the spiritual and civil kingdoms.

Ordinary women found a place of comfort in the church and outnumbered men in general attendance throughout the eighteenth and nineteenth centuries,[26] (calling into question the claims made in *The Earth and Its Peoples*). During the great era of reform, women became active in many church-related charities. That was considered a natural function of their Christian beliefs as well as their innate sensitivity and compassion. In addition, women wrote letters and signed petitions in support of such causes as the abolition of slavery without provoking criticism of their gender. It was public *speaking* that created the uproar. A woman preaching in a public forum might raise eyebrows; however, a woman speaking in public on an issue that had broad political implications brought on a firestorm of criticism, much of it referencing the words of Paul in 1 Corinthians and 1 Timothy. In fact, because of Paul's directives for women to remain silent, these first

26. Degler, *At Odds*, 298–99.

female public speakers often were derided as immoral and irreligious.[27] Clearly, many in the general population at that time (late eighteenth/early nineteenth centuries) still understood the creation ordinances as foundational to a healthy civil society.

One example of this understanding was exhibited during a meeting of the Connecticut State Anti-Slavery Society. A motion had been made that would have excluded women from voting or speaking in the society. When Abby Kelley rose to speak against the motion, the chair ordered her to sit down. His order was over-ruled, and he was infuriated and left with the following retort: "I will not sit in a chair where women bear rule, I vacate that chair. No woman shall speak or vote where I am moderator. I will not countenance such an outrage on decency. I will not consent to have women lord it over men in public assemblies."[28] Similar allusions to 1 Timothy 2 were used repeatedly to denounce the growing number of women speakers in the public arena.

How then did these women defend themselves? Did they brandish their rights to individual self-expression and follow the lead of women like Mary Wollstonecraft and Fanny Wright? No, the genesis of the women's rights movement was anything but self-conscious. It began as a response to being denied the right to exercise God-given moral responsibilities.

Angelina Grimké was among the more articulate of the early American women's rights advocates. Her interest in women's rights grew out of her personal convictions on the issue of slavery. She found that her attempts to exercise

27. O'Connor, *Pioneer Women Orators*, 23.
28. Ibid., 36.

her moral responsibility and speak against chattel slavery in the public square often were thwarted because she was female. In response to these experiences, she developed a theory of human rights that drew on spiritual kingdom language and principles. (Her arguments are notably more biblical than Thomas Jefferson's.) Human beings, according to Grimké, have rights because they are moral beings. In a letter written to Catherine Beecher in 1837, she expressed her thoughts as follows:

> The investigation of the rights of the slave has led me to a better understanding of my own. I have found the Anti-Slavery cause to be the high school of morals in our land—the school in which *human rights* are more fully investigated, and better understood and taught, than in any other. [. . .] Human beings have *rights*, because they are *moral* beings: the rights of *all* men grow out of their moral nature; and as all men have the same moral nature, they have essentially the same rights. These rights may be wrested from the slave but they cannot be alienated [. . .] . Now if rights are founded in the nature of our moral being, then the *mere circumstances of sex* does not give to man higher rights and responsibilities, than to woman. [. . .] When human beings are regarded as *moral* beings, *sex,* instead of being enthroned upon the summit, administering upon rights and responsibilities, sinks into insignificance and nothingness.[29]

Grimké also draws on the spiritual kingdom language of Galatians 3:28: "I recognize no rights but human

29. Grimké, "Letter XII to Catherine Beecher," 320–21.

rights—I know nothing of men's rights and women's rights for in Jesus Christ there is neither male nor female. It is my solemn conviction, that, until this principle of equality is recognized and embodied in practice, the church can do nothing effectual for the permanent reformation of the world."[30]

Again and again at this time in history, we see the gospel and spiritual kingdom values being infused into the political and social culture. Grimké was not some wild-eyed radical, but was speaking a language that resonated with most of the population. In the same letter, she acknowledges that some churches allow women to preach based on "equality in spiritual gifts"; she, however, is addressing something more basic: the issue of human rights.[31] Her primary focus is on the world outside the church, where she believes human rights and moral responsibilities should award to women the same opportunities as men. She also addresses the creation ordinances, on which rest the hierarchies that govern the kingdoms of this world. Grimké makes no reference to 1 Timothy 2, but believes Scripture teaches that woman was created to be man's companion and his equal—"not one hair's breadth beneath him in the majesty and glory of her moral being."[32] Grimké also breathes a spiritual kingdom perspective into the consequences of the fall: "Woman was the first transgressor, and the first victim of power. In all heathen nations, she has been the slave of man, and Christian nations have never acknowledged her

30. Ibid., 322.
31. Ibid.
32. Ibid., 321.

rights."[33] Grimké was appealing to the basic precepts of the spiritual kingdom, just as Luther, Calvin, and the other traditionalists had articulated them; that in Christ there is neither male nor female. The temporal kingdom, as the traditionalists understood it, had been swallowed up by the success of the Protestant Reformation!

In concluding this section, I would like to make a few observations. First of all, the early women's rights movement was no different from the other reform movements of its time. Whether prison reform, temperance, education, abolitionism, or women's rights, they all appealed to spiritual kingdom values and used spiritual kingdom language. That was especially true when women were involved. The meetings of the women's branches of these reform organizations often were conducted like church services, the milieu in which women felt most comfortable and most empowered. Historian Page Smith remarks, "If the Protestant passion was the driving force of American reform, this was most particularly the case in those reform movements dominated by women or in which women were most heavily involved."[34] On the other hand, when women stepped out of the church and into the public arena and began to *speak* and exercise leadership, they often were warned against violating the God-ordained natural order.[35]

I must add that nothing that I read up until the mid-nineteenth century attempted to separate the subordination of women to men from the general idea of rank and social hierarchy. A straightforward reading of Genesis 2 would in-

33. Ibid., 322.
34. Smith, *Daughters of the Promised Land*, 175.
35. Ibid., 101.

dicate that it pertains to husbands and wives only. Yet, not only was it expanded to include the subjection of women to men in general; but, in the popular mind, Genesis 2 laid the biblical basis for all social hierarchies. John C. Calhoun appeals to Genesis 2 in his famous speech on slavery as a positive good.[36] Of course, that was the voice of the temporal kingdom, which was slowly but relentlessly being conquered by the sword of the Spirit.

Evangelicals today who want to distance themselves from the repudiation of the traditional interpretation of 1 Timothy 2:11–14, also must distance themselves from the rise of Puritanism and the First and Second Great Awakenings—and the basic Protestant doctrine of the priesthood of all believers. They may attempt to do this theologically, but it is impossible to do historically. Some might refer to this era as Protestantism against itself—or perhaps as the outworking of a fundamental irony within Protestantism, in that the early reformers were supportive of contemporary social and political hierarchies yet predicated their movement on doctrines that promoted human equality. I have been looking at this period through still another lens: the spiritual kingdom working in tandem with the civil kingdom became the spiritual kingdom versus the civil kingdom. In any event, by the nineteenth century the "Protestant passion" was in the ascendency. Galatians 3:28 superseded the traditional interpretation of 1 Timothy 2. Spiritual kingdom theology shaped the civil kingdom and history, and then in turn, this history shaped theology.

---

36. Calhoun, "Speech on the Oregon Bill," 566.

3

Contemporary Interpretations of 1 Timothy 2:11–14

IN 1874, theologian Patrick Fairbairn (Free Church of Scotland) published a *Commentary on the Pastoral Epistles*, which departs substantially from the traditional exegesis. He begins his discussion of 1 Timothy 2:11–12 by saying that Paul's instructions here are "spoken primarily and mainly with reference to the public assemblies of the church."[1] He makes no application of this passage to the world outside the church. Nevertheless, his somewhat ambiguous use of the phrase "under law" in explaining verse 13 and his reference to the fall in verse 14 as fixing "the social position of woman"[2] indicate he may have held a position similar to Hodge and Ellicott. Consequently, my placement of Fairbairn in the contemporary category is somewhat arbitrary. However, he makes no clear reference to the role of women outside the church, so I have chosen to place him on this side of the great divide.

The shift from traditional to contemporary interpretations of this passage was definitely a nineteenth-century

---

1. Fairbairn, *Commentary on the Pastoral Epistles*, 127.
2. Ibid., 128.

phenomenon, yet it is nuanced and partial among those commentaries that were published between 1850 and 1900. The primary difference between the traditional and contemporary interpretation of 1 Timothy 2 is the removal, in contemporary interpretations, of creation ordinances as foundational to a healthy civil society, at least insofar as they promote the subordination of women to men. Both Hodge and Fairbairn only partially fit either theological criteria. I have chosen to place Fairbairn on this side of the divide because of his initial statement, applying this passage to the role of women in the church.

Over time, what might be described as "the great flip-flop" became complete. Almost all of the commentaries published in the twentieth century onward make no application of creation ordinances to the culture at large. Many go so far as to make creation ordinances organic to the church. The true traditional interpretation says that since male headship / female submission is grounded in creation, it is normative for the cultural at large. Because it is normative for the culture at large, it also is observed in the church. The contemporary "traditional" interpretation says that because male headship / female submission is grounded in creation, it is normative for the church (but not applicable to the culture at large). For instance, the recently published (2008) *English Standard Version Study Bible* explicitly applies these verses to the church only. In the study notes included with the 1 Timothy 2 passage, the commentators support the position that gender roles *in the church* are rooted in the creation order. Elsewhere they remark that this passage does not have "in view the role of women in leadership outside the church (e.g., business or government)."[3] That is hardly what one would call the historic interpretation of this passage. Whether or not it is correct is another question, but it is not the traditional interpretation. Because of this seismic shift in the placement of creation ordinances, it becomes very difficult to make comparisons between the traditional and contemporary interpretations. It is a bit like the proverbial comparison of apples to oranges. I will not attempt an extensive comparison of traditional and contemporary exegeses, but will restrict my comments to a few pertinent observations.

Contemporary commentaries all unite in rejecting (or ignoring) creation ordinances as a basis for a right functioning civil society, at least in regards to the subordination of women to men. Beyond that, they follow a number of trajectories. The prominent Protestant exegetes before the mid-nineteenth century interpreted the 1 Timothy 2 passage in much the same way. That is not true after the nineteenth century. Conservative scholars now wrangle over the meaning of words like *hēsuchia* and *authenteō*, how much to contextualize this passage, how to harmonize this passage with others that appear to be in conflict, the significance of Paul's appeal to Genesis 2–3, and more.

John Stott (Anglican) divides evangelical theologians into three camps on the issue of contextualization: 1) rigid literalism, which fails to distinguish between specific cultural expressions of a principle and the universal principle 2) complete contextualization, which explains the passage solely on the basis of local context, rejecting any universal principles 3) Stott's approach—cultural transposition, which

3. *English Standard Version Study Bible*, 2328.

attempts to distinguish between the timeless principle and the specific cultural expression of that principle, which may differ under varying circumstances.[4]

Stott names no examples to illustrate his first category, although I certainly would place Wayne Grudem, Andreas Köstenberger, George Knight, Douglas Moo, Charles Ryrie, and Thomas R. Schreiner in this camp, the so-called "hierarchists" or "complementarians." Stott cites Gordon Fee's commentary on 1 Timothy and Catherine and Richard Kroeger's book, *I Suffer Not a Woman: Rethinking 1 Timothy 2:11–15 in Light of Ancient Evidence* as examples of the second category, the so-called "evangelical feminists" or "egalitarians." The list also might include Mary J. Evans, Roger Nicole, Philip B. Payne, David Scholer, and Aida Besançon Spencer. Stott's exegesis, which cites the submission/authority antithesis as permanent and universal and the silence/teaching antithesis as a first-century expression that may be changed under different circumstances, is an example of the third. Stott's cultural transposition rubric is an intriguing one although I found few contemporary commentators who adopted this explicit approach to 1 Timothy 2:11–14. Philip Towner is one theologian who handles the passage in a similar way, warning the reader against "easy answers that either simply impose culture on God's will *or* neglect culture altogether."[5]

The true traditional exegesis most definitely contains elements of Stott's cultural transposition. We know from their extensive writings on natural law and the two kingdoms, as well as from the examples we have cited concern-

4. Stott, *Message of I Timothy and Titus*, 75–81.
5. Towner, *1–2 Timothy and Titus*, 81.

ing women in the church, that Luther and Calvin did not root the spiritual kingdom in creation ordinances (and by implication, neither do the other traditional exegetes). Consequently, they do not appeal *directly* to creation ordinances to justify female subordination in the church. Female subordination is conveyed into the church by other intransigent principles. Order (versus confusion) and "decorum" seem to be the universal principles that are cited most often. Luther argues that male headship promotes peace and harmony in the churches.[6] We already have looked at Calvin's position on this issue in our discussion of natural law and the two kingdoms. Another example of Calvin's emphasis on decency and order is found in his exegesis of 1 Corinthians 11:4, where he elaborates in the direction of cultural transposition in his conclusion concerning men and head coverings:

> Paul means nothing more than this—that it should appear that the man has authority, and that the woman is under subjection, and this is secured when the man uncovers his head in the view of the Church, though he should afterwards put on his cap again from fear of catching cold. In fine, the *one* rule to be observed here is το πρέπον—*decorum*. If that is secured, Paul requires nothing further.[7]

Again, the submission/authority antithesis is conveyed into the church through the even broader principles of peaceful worship and appropriate decorum.

6. Luther, "Lectures on I Timothy," 277.
7. Calvin, *Commentary on the Epistles of Paul the Apostle to the Corinthians*, 355.

Matthew Henry's writings imply an understanding of natural law and the two kingdoms similar to Luther and Calvin. However, if we isolate his 1 Corinthians 14 exegesis from this assumption and identify the overriding principle in this passage as female submission to male headship, we still find an exegetical approach clearly based on cultural transposition. Speaking and teaching in public implied "in that age and among that people" an insubordination on the part of women, which, consequently, meant that these activities were prohibited in the church. Henry agrees with Stott that the silence/teaching antithesis is a first-century adaptation of a broader truth. However, he also grounds Paul's admonitions in the intransient principles of decency and propriety.[8] Likewise, Adam Clarke states that Paul's prohibitions in 1 Timothy 2 and 1 Corinthians 14 are primarily addressing disorderly and disobedient conduct in the church. For women to be contending with men in public assemblies of the church was "perfectly indecorous."[9] Although all of these men viewed creation ordinances as the divinely established basis for male headship and female submission (in the temporal kingdom), their first line of appeal in securing female subordination to male headship in the church is order and decorum. One could argue that the traditionalists saw the submission/authority antithesis as a first-century expression of the more universal principles of orderly worship and modest decorum (not dissimilar to today's egalitarian understanding of the 1 Timothy 2 passage). That, however, ignores the traditionalists' views on

8. Henry, *Commentary on the Whole Bible*, see I Corinthians 14:34–35.

9. Clarke, *Matthew to Revelation*, 279.

the prescriptive nature of creation ordinances. So, we have a conundrum: apples and oranges.

Contemporary egalitarian commentators tend to stress environmental factors in Corinth and Ephesus that led Paul to restrict the activities of women in those particular churches.[10] They also refer to the presence of heretics who were influencing "weak-willed women" and the behavior of younger widows who were cavorting from house to house as gossips and "busybodies." (2 Tim 3:1–8, 1 Tim 5:13, NASB) These commentators argue for a local problem, some kind of heresy, which required a local solution. None of the traditional commentators, however, cite these specific problems in Corinth and Ephesus as reasons for Paul's prohibitions.

Also, many egalitarian theologians, such as Gordon Fee (Assemblies of God), believe the proper translation of the word *hēsuchia* is "in a quiet demeanor" not "in silence." In fact, Fee believes the emphasis in the entire passage lies in the need for a quiet demeanor, not silence, on the part of women.[11] In contrast, the traditionalists have no problem with the word "silence" (although all but Gill qualify it).

In addition to the relocation of creation ordinances from the temporal kingdom to the spiritual kingdom, there are other interesting contrasts between the traditional interpretation and contemporary hierarchist interpretations. The vast majority of commentators, including all traditional and many contemporary, give the word *authenteō* a negative connotation—to usurp authority or domineer. In fact,

---

10. For example see Richard Clark Kroeger and Catherine Clark Kroeger, *I Suffer Not a Woman*.

11. Fee, *1 and 2 Timothy, Titus*, 73.

it was not until the mid-twentieth century that I found any theologians (all hierarchists and complementarians) contending for a neutral meaning—to merely exercise authority. (One possible exception would be nineteenth-century exegete Charles Ellicott.) If the historic majority rules, this word has negative connotations; and, consequently, significant implications for the interpretation of the passage.[12] As noted above, the traditionalists all adhered to a negative connotation. Yet, in keeping with their understanding of the differing sources of authority in the civil and spiritual kingdoms, most of the traditionalists acknowledge the possibility of women prophesying/teaching or answering an extraordinary call (i.e., exercising spiritual authority) in the church. Contemporary "traditional" exegetes either ignore or reject this possibility.

A final interesting observation on the differences between the traditional and contemporary interpretations concerns the use of the words "superior" and "inferior." As mentioned before, all the traditional exegetes use these words without apology. The earlier contemporary exegetes also use this language, but it seems to have less to do with social rank and more to do with capacity or merit. (No doubt that has something to do with the drift of Western culture, from a static, hierarchical model to a more fluid "meritocracy.") For instance, Baptist theologian H. Harvey, whose commentary was published in 1890, makes exten-

12. For a list of Bible translations see Belleville, "Teaching and Usurping Authority, 1 Timothy 2:11–15," 209–10. Also see Baldwin, "A Difficult Word: αὐθεντέω in 1Timothy 2:12," 65–80. Also see Philip Payne's discussion of Knight versus Werner in *Man and Woman, One in Christ*, 365–68.

sive use of the word "inferior" to describe woman and "superior" to describe man. However, he uses these words primarily in regards to capacity and merit, and thus adds that the woman shows "superiority to man in those qualities which especially distinguish her within her true sphere."[13] (The idea of separate but complementary spheres was an invention of late eighteenth- and early nineteenth-century popular culture, but it did not receive theological expression until later.) The last enthusiastic reference to male "superiority" in my survey appeared in a 1957 commentary on 1 Timothy written by Edmond Hiebert (Mennonite).[14] From the 1960s onward conservative commentators rushed to use egalitarian language. Baptist theologian Thomas Schreiner's remarks represent the complementarian rejoinder to the assumption that subordination implies female inferiority:

> A difference in role or function does not imply that women are inferior to men. The Son will submit to the Father (1 Cor. 15:28), and yet he is equal to the Father in essence, dignity, and personhood. It is a modern, democratic, Western notion that diverse functions suggest distinctions in worth between men and women. Paul believed that men and women were equal in personhood, dignity, and value but also taught that women had a distinct role from men.[15]

The idea of male/female equality before the throne of grace and equality in personhood, coupled with differing roles or functions in the church, is the position held by

13. Harvey, *Commentary on the Pastoral Epistles*, 35.
14. Hiebert, *First Timothy*, 60.
15. Schreiner, "Interpretation of 1 Timothy 2:9–15," 135–36.

most theologians today who claim to uphold the historic position. That often is coupled with a critique of modern, democratic individualism. Egalitarians seem less inclined towards historical polemics; however, these two voices are not the only ones participating in the conversation.

A recent article in *First Things* identified evangelicals as follows: "the conservative brand of Protestantism reflected by Southern Baptists, the Assemblies of God, the Church of the Nazarene, and others who believe in the final authority of the Bible and the need for conversion."[16] This article had nothing to do with women in the church, but reminds us of the diversity of positions held on this issue within the evangelical community. Most churches that are part of the Holiness and Pentecostal traditions have ordained women from the beginning, and historically the Baptists have certainly produced their share of female preachers. (It should be noted that in all these traditions the numbers of women with an extraordinary call always has been small and has not reflected surrounding cultural norms, which is not the case with the ordination of women in non-evangelical denominations.) Both the Holiness and Pentecostal traditions were born after the early nineteenth century and consequently infuse spiritual kingdom values into their ecclesiastical polity more extensively than do most earlier denominations. An emphasis on the ongoing work of the Holy Spirit also characterizes these traditions.

Interestingly, I found the treatment of 1 Timothy 2:11–14 in *The Wesleyan's Bible Commentary*, published in 1965, to be closer to the true traditional exegesis than perhaps any other. The author, Roy S. Nicholson, who frequently

16. Johnson, "Good News About Evangelicalism," 12.

paraphrases Clarke, states that the Bible clearly establishes a chain of command (1 Cor 11). When commenting on 1 Timothy 2:11, he says "the question at issue here is that of order in the public worship service."[17] At this point, he takes the typical contemporary position, applying this verse to public worship in the church only. He leans in an egalitarian direction by suggesting the primary concern of the apostle here was order. Women, who were poorly educated at the time and may have been influenced by heresy, were disrupting the worship services with inappropriate questions.[18] However, in treating verse 12, he says, "This principle [that women should not usurp authority] reaches beyond the congregation of Christian worshipers to the entire community," a position reminiscent of the traditional exegesis—but in 1965! Nicholson ends his discussion (verse 13) by basing what he earlier referred to as a "chain of subordination" in creation ordinances.[19] He does not, however, tie his rather divergent ideas together into a consistent worldview concerning the role of women in church and society, leaving the reader somewhat bewildered. A comprehensible natural law / two kingdoms framework is missing.

Within Holiness church polity, there are also hints of the traditional spiritual kingdom / civil kingdom view. In 1985, for instance, the Church of the Nazarene issued a statement affirming the spiritual equality of women and men, based on Galatians 3:28, which they believe has functional implications within the church. Consequently, they affirm the right of women to exercise God-given spiritual

17. Nicholson, "I Timothy & II Timothy and Titus," 585.
18. Ibid.
19. Ibid.

gifts within the church. However, the statement also strongly recognizes the God-given distinctions between men and women and says, "Therefore, we oppose any legislation which would be against the scriptural teaching of the place of womanhood in society."[20] Thus, there are many voices in the conversation, and the post-nineteenth-century discussion on the interpretation and application of 1 Timothy 2 continues.

It seems appropriate to close this section with a closer examination of what I have called the "great flip-flop"—the transposition of creation ordinances from the civil kingdom into the spiritual. The following three quotations are excellent examples of the discontinuity between the authentic traditional interpretation and contemporary interpretations, in spite of claims to the contrary:

1. J. I. Packer (Anglican) writes "that the man-woman relationship is intrinsically non-reversible [. . .]. This is part of the reality of creation, a given fact that nothing will change. Certainly, redemption will not change it, for grace restores nature, not abolishes it."[21] This is the presupposition on which many contemporary theologians build their exegeses.

2. John MacArthur (Reformed, nondenominational) says the following in his commentary on 1 Timothy 2: "Those who insist that subordination and equality are mutually exclusive would do well to consider Christ's relationship to the Father. While on earth, Jesus assumed a subordinate role, yet He was in no way in-

20. See *Manual of the Church of the Nazarene*, 283.
21. Packer, "Understanding the Differences," 299.

ferior. First Corinthians 11:3 states, 'But I want you to understand that Christ is the head of every man, and the man is the head of the woman, and God is the head of Christ.'"[22] Later MacArthur clearly states that male headship applies to the church only. In commenting on spiritual gifts, he says, "It does not mean that women do not have spiritual gifts in the area of public speaking and leadership. The issue is where they exercise those gifts."[23]

3. In the book, *Women in the Church, A Fresh Analysis of 1 Timothy 2:9–15*, Daniel Doriani (Presbyterian) includes an historical survey of this passage in the appendix, not dissimilar to what I have done. However, his conclusions are quite different. He writes, "Throughout the ages the church has traditionally interpreted 1 Timothy 2:11–14 in a straightforward manner. This book has presented extensive data to demonstrate that the traditional reading is correct."[24] He then goes on to summarize that traditional reading. Included in his summary is the following statement: "For complementarians, the phrase, 'Adam was formed or created first,' refers beyond chronology to God's sovereign decree that made males the spiritual heads of God's kingdom, churches, and homes."[25]

I hope, by this time, the reader is able to identify how the above statements digress from the traditional view.

22. MacArthur, *I Timothy*, 86.
23. Ibid., 87.
24. Doriani, "Appendix I," 262.
25. Ibid.

The key, of course, is an understanding of the natural law and two-kingdoms worldview. Within this traditional framework, grace is foundational to the spiritual kingdom and does not "restore nature" in the sense implied above. (Creational laws of nature are foundational to the God-ordained, but separate, civil kingdom). Being rooted in creation ordinances, male headship and female subordination cannot be abrogated in the temporal world—which would include a ban on female public speaking and leadership. Galatians 3:28 expresses the overriding principle in the spiritual kingdom, represented on earth by the church. The traditionalists (such as John Calvin) clearly reject the above exegesis of 1 Corinthians 11 and state that the *spiritual* head of woman is Christ alone. Male headship is fundamental to the temporal kingdom. Out of respect for propriety and accepted social decorum, it is honored in the church. Whether the authentic traditional interpretation is the correct interpretation is another question altogether. However, I hope that my efforts to clarify the traditional position have added some new and useful information to the ongoing conversation.

4

Where Do We Go From Here?

IN CLOSING, I would like to muse on a few possible implications of this study for future research and discussion. We are peering at a very large subject (the roles of men and women in church and culture) through a very small window (the historic interpretation of 1 Timothy 2). The last word on this subject has not been written.

If Luther, Calvin, Poole, Henry, Gill, Scott, Wesley, and Clarke were here today, what would they say about 1 Timothy 2:11–14 and the tremendous changes that have taken place in Western culture since they reflected on this passage? That involves more speculation than I care to indulge in; however, we can apply the core of the traditional interpretation to today's world with a degree of confidence. A true traditionalist today would work to re-instate creation ordinances as regards men and women in the civil kingdom. S/he would do this with the same vigor evangelicals demonstrate in opposing gay marriage—and for the same reason, the application of creation ordinances to the civil kingdom. If a nation is to flourish, it should base its civil law on God-ordained natural law, which teaches male headship / female subordination and heterosexual marriage. A true traditionalist would work to remove women from positions of leadership and authority in government, business, and the academy, regardless of ideology. The traditional view also would have implications for female education. Why encourage daughters to pursue careers that might place them in positions of authority over men? Even without a sophisticated two-kingdom perspective, there is a simple logic to the traditional position. If creation ordinances are universally binding, then they should be applied to *all* creation. A true traditionalist would see some of our modern-day malaise as a byproduct of the increasing numbers of women exercising leadership in the culture at large. However, given the nature of Western society today, the true traditionalist would have a challenge. S/he would need to present male headship/female subordination in such a way that men and women would *choose* to live their lives within this framework. Passing laws to restrict female participation in the political culture, for instance, would be unlikely. (On the other hand, within the life of the church, a true traditionalist might be open to women leading, in accordance to the promptings of the Holy Spirit.) However, there are no, or few, true traditionalists today and that, too, has implications.

Complementarians and others who claim to uphold the historic position on 1 Timothy 2 need to either make major exegetical adjustments and embrace the traditionalist position in full, or acknowledge the significant differences between their exegeses and pre-nineteenth-century understandings. The authentic traditional interpretation of 1 Timothy 2 shares some things in common with today's complementarians and some things in common with today's egalitarians. However, neither of these contemporary interpretative frameworks have enough in common with the authentic traditional exegesis to claim to be the heir of that tradition. It is disingenuous to make that claim. (In fact, one could argue that today's egalitarians are closer to the traditional position, in that, like the traditionalists, they understand the fundamental principles in the spiritual kingdom/church to be egalitarian. Most traditionalists also held that these principles had possible functional implications.) Theologians need to do some honest re-thinking here, so the conversation can continue on a level playing field. This issue also highlights the unfortunate disconnect that sometimes exists between theologians and Christian historians.

VanDrunen's book is primarily a history, yet it demonstrates an obvious breadth of theological expertise. Both disciplines, history and theology, were needed to inform such a detailed and scholarly work. Unfortunately, many theologians seem all too ready to make historical judgments without much accurate information. Theologian Robert Yarborough, for instance, in writing about the hermeneutics of 1 Timothy 2, associates the modern feminist movement with contemporary, autonomous individualism. So far, so good. He traces its roots back through existentialism, utilitarianism, Marxism, and "liberalism" (meaning the elevation of individual rights over social and institutionally mandated moral and civic responsibilities). He then goes on to say that "the 'first wave' [of feminism] arose in the late 1700s, a spin-off from the rise of liberalism itself."[1] All his sources appear to be philosophical and theological. An historically informed opinion would have drawn a much

1. Yarborough, "Hermeneutics of 1 Timothy 2:9–15," 161.

different picture of first wave feminism (see previous discussion of Angelina Grimké). The religious individualism implicit in Protestantism was largely responsible for the advance of such Western distinctives as equality under the law, representative government, and the defense of human rights based on concepts of individual worth, even when these principles were applied to women. To deny this is to attach the "train" of Western civilization to the wrong engine. How and when the train came off the tracks is a separate, although not unrelated, question.

No doubt we need more "cross-pollination" between historians and theologians in the Christian community. Unfortunately for some theologians, real history, like real people, is nuanced and rarely accommodates a good guy versus bad guy approach. Secular historians, on the other hand, often discount theology. Many in the past have failed, for instance, to make the connection between popular religion and the various reform movements of the late eighteenth and nineteenth centuries.[2] It is alarming when Christian theologians contribute to this misinformation. Regrettably, the problem in both camps is often about shooting arrows first and then painting targets. On the one hand, well-meaning theologians want to distance evangelicalism from the rise of modern individualism, and on the other hand, secular historians also want to distance evangelicalism from the rise of modern individualism—the former because they see modern individualism as a bad

2. Social historian Lawrence Stone (1919–1999) is one example of a prominent scholar who failed to make the connection. Fortunately, this deficit is being addressed by contemporary historians, such as Catherine Brekus, Timothy Larsen, and Mark Noll.

thing and the latter because they see it as a good thing! So, truth goes wanting. In the interest of academic integrity, I believe a more academically integrated approach should be taken in future discussions of the historic interpretation of 1 Timothy 2:11–14 and the role of women in the church.

This study also raises another, more esoteric concern about the relationship between history and theology. How do we talk about the ongoing work of the Holy Spirit in history? Do we recognize the work of the Holy Spirit in the many conversions that took place during the Great Awakening but not in the egalitarian impulses that accompanied those conversions? Do we recognize the anti-slavery movement as a work inspired by the Holy Spirit, but not the women's rights movement? Should we even presume anything about God's work in history, beyond what is explicitly stated in Scripture? Was the Christianization of culture during the seventeenth, eighteenth, and nineteenth centuries truly a work of the Holy Spirit, or did it result in an unfortunate conflagration of church and state? Most likely there were elements of both. How do we talk about these things? The popular solution seems to be to restrict discussions to "church" history, which enables us to talk about the importance of the spiritual, yet avoids identifying the specific ways that God has been at work. Yet in our personal lives we confirm God's ongoing work. Why not in our corporate lives? Is the natural law and two kingdoms paradigm the way God desires to deal with humanity? Or is our mission as Christians to bring spiritual kingdom values to bear on all of culture? None of these questions are new. There are no easy answers, but this study, particularly as it identified the tremendous influence nineteenth-century history had on subsequent biblical scholarship, raises these questions again. Conservative theologians cannot afford to be dismissive of history, as they, too, are products of it. Likewise, historians need help in knowing how to talk about God's work in extra-biblical history, without being presumptuous or sacrificing "academic objectivity."

Finally, I would like to respond to a question that was raised at the beginning of this monograph: Has Christianity promoted male domination in the church? Or, at least, what can we say about male domination in the church using the limited vantage point of this particular research project? The answer, as to whether Christianity has promoted male dominance, has to be "yes" and "no." First of all, men always have occupied the vast majority of leadership positions in the church, from the beginning. Even in the evangelical world among denominations that have given greater latitude to egalitarian spiritual kingdom principles, the number of women in leadership always has been small. Yet, from the beginning of Protestantism, and even before (Waldensians, Hussites), there have been women who have answered an extraordinary call. This was *contra mundum* before the nineteenth century, in that there were any women exercising spiritual leadership at all. And yet, it is still *contra mundum* today, in that the numbers are so small. So then, we can answer the question with a "yes." Men always have occupied most leadership positions in the church, and we have read numerous explanations as to why that is so. However, in terms of sheer numbers, women often have, if not always, dominated.[3]

---

3. See comments on the ratio of women to men in the early church in Stark, *The Rise of Christianity*, 110–15.

In regards to our study here, I would like to focus on the question: Did the traditional exegetes promote male domination in the church? In a limited sense, we can say "No, they did not." The traditional exegetes associated male dominance with creation ordinances and the civil kingdom. In the world in which they lived, that was a given. In contrast, the spiritual kingdom, represented by the church, ultimately operated under different principles. Christianity, particularly the Protestant emphasis on salvation by *grace* through faith, has an egalitarian core. No other major world religion has a central doctrine like the priesthood of *all* believers, women as well as men. Again, it may be possible to build a theological argument against these doctrines having functional implications; however, that would be impossible to do historically, because they clearly did. Are these doctrines what attracted women to Christianity? Or, were women attracted to Christianity because of the predominance of male leadership? The answer must lie in the former, not the latter. Before the nineteenth century, the church, particularly in its evangelical Protestant form, empowered women who had been transformed by God's grace in ways that were unheard of in other times and places. That was something new under the sun. So, no, *spiritual* kingdom values did not promote male dominance in the church. In fact, I would argue that as regards the status of women in Western culture, spiritual kingdom values were a major source of Western exceptionalism. Therefore, in this sense, we can say that Christianity is unique among all the major world religions, in the way it has elevated the position of women.

This yes-and-no equivocation perhaps reflects the tension inherent in the church's understanding of the kingdom of God. After all, the coming of the kingdom is an already-but-not-yet phenomenon, and we must live in that tension. Some will give realized eschatology larger scope than others. This is true now, and was true in the past. I only hope that in discussing these issues in the future we can give each other grace, and encourage the conversation to go on with mutual charity and respect. In the words of John Calvin, "Let not church despise church because of a difference in external discipline."[4]

---

4. Calvin, *Institutes*, 4.10.32.

Appendix

Excerpts from Luther's "Temporal Authority" and Calvin's Institutes

THE FOLLOWING are excerpts taken from Luther's "Temporal Authority: To What Extent It Should Be Obeyed" (edited by Walther I. Brandt). Note the distinctions Luther makes between the spiritual and temporal kingdoms and the principles that govern these kingdoms, especially those precepts that are foundational to the spiritual kingdom/church. Also note the context in which he uses the word "external."

> Third. Here we must divide the children of Adam and all mankind into two classes, the first belonging to the kingdom of God, the second to the kingdom of the world. Those who belong to the kingdom of God are the true believers who are in Christ and under Christ, for Christ is King and Lord in the kingdom of God, as Psalm 2 [:6] and all of Scripture says. For this reason he came into the world, that he might begin God's kingdom and establish it in the world. Therefore, he says before Pilate, "My kingdom is not of this world, but every one who is of the truth hears my voice" [John 18:36–37]. In the gospel he continually

refers to the kingdom of God, and says, "Amend your ways, the kingdom of God is at hand" [Matt 4:17, 10:7]; again, "Seek first the kingdom of God and his righteousness" [Matt 6:33]. He also calls the gospel a gospel of the kingdom of God; because it teaches, governs, and upholds God's kingdom. (88)

Now observe, these people need no temporal law or sword. If all the world were composed of real Christians, that is, true believers, there would be no need or benefits from prince, lord, sword, or law. They would serve no purpose, since Christians have in their heart the Holy Spirit, who both teaches and makes them do injustice to no one, to love everyone, and to suffer injustice and even death willingly and cheerfully at the hands of anyone. Where there is nothing but the unadulterated doing of right and bearing of wrong, there is no need of any suit, litigation, court, judge, penalty, law, or sword. For this reason it is impossible that the temporal sword or law should find any work to do among Christians, since they do of their own accord much more than all laws and teachings can demand, just as Paul says in 1 Timothy 1 [:9], "The law is not laid down for the just, but for the lawless." (89)

Fourth. All who are not Christians belong to the kingdom of the world and are under the law. There are few true believers, and even fewer who live a Christian life, who do not resist evil and indeed themselves do no evil. For this reason God has provided for them a different government beyond the Christian estate and kingdom of God. He has subjected them to the sword so that, even though they would like to, they are unable to practice their wickedness, and if they do practice it they cannot do so without fear or with success and impunity. (90)

If anyone attempted to rule the world by the gospel and to abolish all temporal law and sword on the plea that all are baptized and Christian, and that, according to the gospel, there shall be among them no law or sword—or need for either—pray tell me, friend, what would he be doing? He would be loosing the ropes and chains of the savage wild beasts and letting them bite and mangle everyone, meanwhile insisting that they were harmless, tame, and gentle creatures; but I would have the proof in my wounds. Just so would the wicked under the name of Christian abuse evangelical freedom, carry on their rascality, and insist that they were Christians subject neither to law or sword, as some are already raving and ranting.

To such a one we must say: Certainly it is true that Christians, so far as they themselves are concerned, are subject neither to law or sword, and have need of neither. But take heed and first fill the world with real Christians before you attempt to rule it in a Christian and evangelical manner. This you will never accomplish; for the world and the masses are and always will be un-Christian, even if they are all baptized and Christian in name. [. . .] Therefore, it is out of the question that there should be a common Christian government over the whole world, or indeed over a single country or any considerable body of people, for the wicked always outnumber the good. (91)

For this reason one must carefully distinguish between these two governments. Both must be permitted to remain; the one to produce righteousness, the other to produce external peace and prevent evil deeds. Neither one is sufficient in the world without the other. No one can become righteous in the sight of God by means of the temporal government, without Christ's spiritual government. (92)

It is to be noted first that the two classes of Adam's children—the one in God's kingdom under Christ and the other in the kingdom of the world under the governing authority, as was said above—have two kinds of laws. For every kingdom must have its own laws and statutes; without law no kingdom or government can survive, as everyday experience amply shows. The temporal government has laws which extend no further than to life and property and external affairs on earth, for God cannot and will not permit anyone but himself to rule over the soul. Therefore, when the temporal government presumes to prescribe laws for the soul, it encroaches on God's government and only misleads souls and destroys them. (105)

Now you have just heard that no one but God can have authority over souls. Hence, St. Paul cannot possibly be speaking of any obedience except where there can be corresponding authority. From this it follows that he is not speaking of faith, to the effect that temporal authority should have the right to command faith. He is speaking rather of external things, that they should be ordered and governed on earth. His words too make this perfectly clear, where he prescribes limits for both authority and obedience, saying, "Pay all of them their dues, taxes whom taxes are due, revenue to whom revenue is due, honor to whom honor is due, respect to whom respect is due" [Rom 13:7]. Temporal obedience and authority, you see, apply only externally to taxes, revenue, honor, and respect. Again, where he says, "The governing authority is not a terror to good conduct, but to bad" [Rom 13:3], he again so limits the governing authority that it is not to have the mastery over faith or the word of God, but over evil works. (110)

David too summarized all this long ago in an excellent brief passage, when he said in Psalm 113 [115:16], "He has given heaven to the Lord of heaven, but the earth he has given to the sons of men." That is, over what is on earth and belongs to the temporal, earthy kingdom, man has authority from God; but whatever belongs to heaven and the eternal kingdom is exclusively under the Lord of heaven. Neither did Moses forget this when he said in Genesis 1 [:26], "God said, 'Let us make man to have dominion over the beasts of the earth, the fish of the sea, and the birds of the air.'" There only external dominion is ascribed to man. In short, this is the meaning as St. Peter says in Acts 4 [5:29], "We must obey God rather than men." Thereby, he clearly sets a limit to the temporal authority, for if we had to do everything that the temporal authority wanted there would have been no point in saying, "We must obey God rather than men." (111)

But you might say, "Since there is no temporal sword among Christians, how then are they to be ruled outwardly? There certainly must be authority even among Christians." Answer: Among Christians there shall and can be no authority; rather all alike are to be subject to one another, as Paul says in Romans 12: "Each shall consider the other his superior"; and Peter says in 1 Peter 5 [:5], "All of you be subject to one another." This is also what Christ means in Luke 14 [:10], "When you are invited to a wedding, go and sit in the lowest place." Among Christians there is no superior but Christ himself, and him alone. What kind of authority can there be where all are equal and have the same right, power, possession, and honor, and where no one desires to be the other's superior, but each one the other's subordinate? Where there are such people, one could not establish authority even if he wanted to, since in the nature of things it is impossible to have superiors where no one is able or willing to be a superior. Where there are no such people, however, there are no real Christians either.

What, then, are the priests and bishops? Answer: Their government is not a matter of authority or power, but a service and an office, for they are neither higher nor better than any other Christians. Therefore, they should impose no law or decree on others without their consent. Their ruling is rather nothing more than the inculcating of God's word, by which they guide Christians and overcome heresy. As we have said, Christians can be ruled by nothing except God's word, for Christians must be ruled in faith, not with outward works. (117)

Appendix

The following excerpts are all taken from Calvin's *Institutes* (Beveridge translation). The first part is taken from Book 3, Chapter 19 and the next from Book 4, Chapter 20. Note the distinctions Calvin makes between the temporal and spiritual kingdoms and how they relate to each other. Also note his use of the word "external." At the end, I have included one example of Calvin's references to natural law as the basis for civil laws.

> Since by means of this privilege of liberty which we have described, believers have derived authority from Christ not to entangle themselves by the observance of things in which he wished them to be free, we conclude that their consciences are exempted from all human authority. For it were unbecoming for the gratitude due to Christ for his liberal gift should perish, or that the consciences of believers should derive no benefit from it. We must not regard it as a trivial matter when we see how much it cost our Saviour, being purchased not with silver or gold but with his own blood (1 Pet 1:18, 19); so that Paul hesitates not to say that Christ has died in vain, if we place our souls under subjection to men (Gal 5:1, 4; 1 Cor 7:23). Several chapters of the Epistle to the Galatians are wholly occupied with showing that Christ is obscured, or rather extinguished to us, unless our consciences maintain their liberty; from which they have certainly fallen, if they can be bound with the chains of laws and constitutions at the pleasure of men. But as the knowledge of this subject is of the greatest importance, so it demands a longer and clearer exposition. (3.19.14)

Therefore, lest this prove a stumbling block to any, let us observe that in man government is twofold: the one spiritual by which the conscience is trained to piety and divine worship; the other civil by which the individual is instructed in those duties which, as men and citizens, we are bound to perform (see 4.10.3–6). To these two forms are commonly given the not inappropriate names of spiritual and temporal jurisdiction, intimating that the former species has reference to the life of the soul, while the latter relates to matters of the present life, not only to food and clothing, but to the enacting of laws which require a man to live among his fellows purely, honourably, and modestly. [. . .] By attending to this distinction, we will not erroneously transfer the doctrine of the gospel concerning spiritual liberty to civil order, as if in regard to external government Christians were less subject to human laws, because their consciences are unbound before God, as if they were exempted from all carnal service, because in regard to the Spirit they are free. (3.19.15)

Having shown above that there is a twofold government in man, and having fully considered the one which, placed in the soul or inward man, relates to eternal life, we are called here to say something of the other, which pertains to civil institutions and the external regulation of manners. [. . .] For some, on hearing that liberty is promised in the gospel, a liberty that acknowledges no king and no magistrate among men, but looks to Christ alone, think that they can receive no benefit from their liberty so long as they see any power placed over them. Accordingly, they think that nothing will be safe until the whole world is changed into a new form, when there will be neither courts, nor laws, nor magistrates, nor anything of the kind to interfere, as they suppose, with their liberty. But he who knows to distinguish between the body and the soul, between the present fleeting life and that which is future and eternal, will have no difficulty in understanding that the spiritual kingdom of Christ and civil government are things very widely separated. [. . .] For why is it that the very same apostle who bids us "stand fast in the liberty wherewith Christ hath made us free, and be not entangled with the yoke of bondage" (Gal 5:1), in another passage forbids slaves to be solicitous about their state (1 Cor 7:21), unless it be that spiritual liberty is perfectly compatible with civil servitude? In this sense the following passages are to be understood: "There is neither Jew nor Greek, there is neither bond nor free, there is neither male nor female" (Gal 3:28). Again, "There is neither Greek nor Jew, circumcision nor uncircumcision, barbarian, Scythian, bond nor free: but Christ is all and in all" (Col 3:11). It is thus intimated, that it matters not what your condition is among men, nor under what laws you live, since in them the kingdom of Christ does not at all consist.

Still the distinction does not go so far as to justify us in supposing that the whole scheme of civil government is matter of pollution, with which Christian men have nothing to do. [. . .] But as we lately taught that that kind of government is distinct from the spiritual and internal kingdom of Christ, so we ought to know that they are not adverse to each other. The former [spiritual], in some measure, begins the heavenly kingdom in us, even now upon earth, and in this mortal and evanescent life commences immortal and incorruptible blessedness, while to the latter [civil] it is assigned, so long as we live among men, to foster and maintain the external worship of God, to defend sound doctrine and the condition of the Church, to adapt our conduct to human society, to form our manners to civil justice, to conciliate us to each other, to cherish common peace and tranquility. (4.20.1–2)

What I have said will become plain if we attend, as we ought to two things connected with all laws—viz. the enactment of the law, and the equity on which the enactment is founded and rests. Equity, as it is natural, cannot be the same in all, and therefore ought to be proposed by all laws, according to the nature of the thing enacted. As constitutions have some circumstances on which they partly depend, there is nothing to prevent their diversity, provided they all alike aim at equity as their end. Now, as it is evident that the law of God which we call moral, is nothing else than the testimony of natural law, and of the conscience that God has engraven on the minds of men, the whole of this equity of which we now speak is prescribed in it. Hence it alone ought to be the aim, the rule, and the end of all laws. Wherever laws are formed after this rule, directed to this aim, and restricted to this end, there is no reason why they should be disapproved of by us, however much they differ from Jewish law, or from each other. (4.20.16).

The above was written in the context of Calvin's discussion of the civil kingdom and civil laws. The following are excerpts taken from Book 4, chapter 10 and address the principles that should guide ecclesiastical government. Notice how Calvin treats Paul's prohibition against women teaching *in the church*. He clearly does not see this prohibition as a timeless principle established by creation ordinances and Eve's role in the fall. Rather, he appeals to order, custom, and the edification of the church.

> . . . that in the sacred assembly of the faithful, all things may be done decently, and with becoming dignity, and that human society may be maintained in order by certain bonds, as it were, of moderation and humanity. [. . .] But it may be proper to explain more clearly what is meant by the decency which Paul commends, and also what is comprehended under order. And the object of decency is, partly that by the use of rites, which produce reverence in sacred matters, we may be excited to piety, and partly that the modesty and gravity which ought to be seen in all honourable actions may here especially be conspicuous. In order, the first thing is, that those who preside know the law and rule of right government, while those who are governed be accustomed to obedience and right discipline. The second thing is, by arranging the state of the Church, provision be made for peace and tranquility. (4.10.28)
>
> Of the former class [decency], we have examples (1 Cor 11:5, 21), where Paul says profane entertainments must not be intermingled with the sacred Supper of the Lord; that women must not

appear in public uncovered. And there are many other things which we have in daily practice, such as praying on our knees, and with our head uncovered, administering the sacraments of the Lord, not sordidly, but with some degree of dignity; employing some degree of solemnity in the burial of our dead, and so forth. In the other class [order] are the hours set aside for public prayer, sermon, and solemn services; during sermon, quiet and silence, fixed places, singing of hymns, days set apart for the celebration of the Lord's Supper, the prohibition of Paul against women teaching in the Church, and such like. [. . .] Thus all ecclesiastical constitutions, which we admit to be sacred and salutary, may be reduced to two heads, the one relating to rites and ceremonies, the other to discipline and peace. (4.10.29)

But as there is here a danger, on the one hand, lest false bishops should thence derive a pretext for their impious and tyrannical laws, and on the other, lest some, too apt to take alarm, should from fear of the above evils, leave no place for laws, however, holy, it may here be proper to declare, that I approve of those human constitutions only which are founded on the authority of God, and are derived from Scripture, and are therefore altogether divine. Let us take, for example, the bending of the knee which is made in public prayer. It is asked, whether this is a human tradition, which any one is at liberty to repudiate or neglect? I say, that it is human, and at the same time it is divine. It is of God, inasmuch as it is a part of decency, the care and observance of which is recommended by the apostle; and it is of men, inasmuch as it specially determines what was indicated in general, rather than expounded. From this one example, we may judge what is to be thought of the whole class—viz. that the whole sum of righteousness, and all the parts of divine worship, and everything necessary to salvation, the Lord has faithfully comprehended, and clearly unfolded, in his sacred oracles, so that in them he alone is the only Master to be heard. But as in external discipline and ceremonies, he has not been pleased to prescribe every particular that we are to observe (he foresaw that this depended on the nature of the times, and that one form would not suit all ages), in them we must have recourse to the general rules which he has given, employing them to test whatever the necessity of the Church may require to be enjoined for order and decency. Lastly, he has not delivered any express command, because things of this nature are not necessary to salvation, and for the edification of the Church, should be accommodated to the varying circumstances of each age and nation; it will be proper, as the interest of the Church may require, to change and abrogate the old, as well as to introduce new forms. [. . .] Charity is the best judge of what tends to hurt or edify: if we allow her to be the guide, all things will be safe. (4.10.30)

Things which have been appointed according to this rule, it is the duty of the Christian people to observe with a free conscience indeed, and without superstition, but also with a pious and ready inclination to obey. [. . .] You will ask, What liberty of conscience will there be in such cautious observances? Nay, this liberty will admirably appear when we shall hold that these are not fixed and perpetual obligations to which we are astricted, but external rudiments for human infirmity, which, though we do not all need, we, however, all use, because we are bound to cherish mutual charity towards each other. This we may recognize in the examples given above. What? Is religion placed in a woman's bonnet, so that it is unlawful for her to go out with her head uncovered? Is her silence fixed by a decree which cannot be violated without the greatest wickedness? Is there any mystery in bending the knee, or in burying a dead body, which cannot be omitted without a crime? By no means. For if a woman require to make such haste in assisting a neighbour that she has not time to cover her head, she sins not in running out with her head uncovered. And there are some occasions on which it is not less seasonable for her to speak than on others to be silent. Nothing, moreover, forbids him who, from disease, cannot bend his knees, to pray standing. In fine, it is better to bury a dead man quickly, than for want of grave-clothes, or the absence of those who should attend the funeral, to wait till it rot away unburied. Nevertheless, in those matters the custom and institutions of the country, in short, humanity and the rules of modesty itself, declare what is to be done or avoided. [. . .] For what a seed-bed of quarrels will confusion in such matters be, if every one is allowed at pleasure to alter what pertains to common order? (4.10.31)

The effect of this procedure is, that in all these matters each retains his freedom, and yet at the same time voluntarily subjects it to a kind of necessity, in so far as the *decency* of which we have spoken or charity demands. Next, that in the observance of these things we may not fall into any superstition, nor rigidly require too much from others, let us not imagine that the worship of God is improved by a multitude of ceremonies: let not church despise church because of a difference in external discipline. Lastly, instead of here laying down any perpetual law for ourselves, let us refer the whole end and use of observances to the edification of the Church, at whose request let us without offence allow not only something to be changed, but even observances which were formerly in use to be inverted. (4.10.32)

1 TIMOTHY 2 APPENDIX DISCUSSION QUESTIONS

Women's history cannot be separated from the general rise of representative government, human rights, and equality under the law in the modern, Western world. Likewise, the Protestant Reformation played a vital role in laying the foundation for these Western distinctives. The following questions are designed to help students of women's history and Western history make connections between ideas and consequences, in their immediate and long term sociopolitical context.

Luther

1. List the principles by which Luther says the church should operate.
2. Keep in mind that Luther was writing at the very dawn of the modern age—at a time when civil society was static and hierarchal in nature. How might Luther's ideas have inspired democratic aspirations among the people?
3. Define the word "external," according to Luther's usage.
4. Describe Luther's position on applying the principles that animate the church / spiritual kingdom to government and civil society. Do you think Luther would have supported the movement to abolish slavery in the nineteenth century? Why or why not?
5. Research the Peasants' War in Germany (1524–25). How might Luther's ideas have inspired this uprising? What was Luther's response to the Peasants' War?

Calvin

1. According to Calvin, what are the basic principles by which the church should operate?
2. Based on all you have read, in his exegeses and *Institutes* how would you describe Calvin's position on women teaching in the church?
3. Define the word "external," according to Calvin's usage.
4. What do you think Calvin's position on the "divine right" of kings would have been?

Appendix 91

5. Based on all you have read on Calvin's ideas concerning natural law and the civil kingdom, do you think he would have supported the movement to abolish slavery in the nineteenth century? Why or why not?

6. In what ways did Calvin believe in religious toleration?

7. Read about Calvin's conflict with and eventual execution of Miguel Servetus (Geneva, 1553). Were Calvin's actions consistent with his ideas concerning the two kingdoms? Why or why not?

Bibliography

Anderson, Olive. "Women Preachers in Mid-Victorian Britain: Some Reflections on Feminism, Popular Religion, and Social Change." *Historical Journal* 12 (1967) 467–84.

Baldwin, H. Scott. "A Difficult Word: αὐθεντέω in 1 Timothy 2:12." In *Women in the Church: A Fresh Analysis of 1 Timothy 2:9–15*, edited by Andreas J. Köstenberger et al., 65–80. Grand Rapids: Baker, 2000.

Barclay, Robert. *An Apology for the True Christian Divinity*. Glenside, PA: Quaker Heritage Press, 2002. Online: http://www.qhpress.org/texts/barclay/apology/index.html.

Barclay, William. *The Letters to Timothy, Titus, and Philemon*. Rev ed. Philadelphia: Westminster, 1975.

Barzun, Jacques. *From Dawn to Decadence, 1500 to Present: 500 Years of Western Cultural Life*. 1st Harper Perennial ed. New York: HarperCollins, 2001.

Baxter, Richard. *The Reformed Pastor*. Edited by William Brown. Aylesbury, UK: Hazel, Watson, and Viney, 1829.

Belleville, Linda L. "Teaching and Usurping Authority, 1 Timothy 2:11–15" In *Discovering Biblical Equality: Complementarity Without Hierarchy*, edited by Ronald W. Pierce et al., 205–223. Downers Grove, IL: InterVarsity, 2004.

Bray, Gerald. *Biblical Interpretation, Past and Present*. Downers Grove, IL: InterVarsity, 1996.

Brekus, Catherine A. *Strangers and Pilgrims: Female Preaching in America, 1740–1845*. Chapel Hill: University of North Carolina Press, 1998.

Calhoun, John C. "Speech on the Oregon Bill." In *Union and Liberty: The Political Philosophy of John C. Calhoun*. Indianapolis: Liberty Fund, 1992.

Calvin, John. *Commentaries on the Epistles to Timothy, Titus, and Philemon*. Translated by William Pringle. Vol. 21, *Calvin's Commentaries*. Grand Rapids: Baker, 1981.

———. *Commentary on the Epistles of Paul the Apostle to the Corinthians*. Translated by John Pringle. Vol. 20, *Calvin's Commentaries*. Grand Rapids: Baker, 1981.

Calvin, John. *Institutes of the Christian Religion*, 2 vols. Translated by Henry Beveridge. Grand Rapids: Eerdmans, 1970.

Clarke, Adam. *The New Testament of Our Lord and Savior Jesus Christ*. Vol. 3, *Matthew to Revelation*. Nashville: Abingdon, 1977.

Degler, Carl N. *At Odds: Women and the Family in America from the Revolution to the Present*. Oxford: Oxford University Press, 1980.

Doriani, Daniel. "Appendix 1: A History of the Interpretation of I Timothy 2." In *Women in the Church: A Fresh Analysis of 1 Timothy 2:9–15*, edited by Andreas J. Köstenberger et al., 213–67. Grand Rapids: Baker, 2000.

Earle, Ralph. "1 Timothy." *Ephesians–Philemon*. Vol. 11, *The Expositor's Bible Commentary*, edited by Frank E. Gaebelein. Grand Rapids: Zondervan, 1996.

Ellicott, Charles John. *A Critical and Grammatical Commentary on the Pastoral Epistles*. Boston: Draper and Halliday, 1867.

———, editor. *Ellicott's Commentary on the Whole Bible*. Vol. 8, *Ephesians–Revelations*. Grand Rapids: Zondervan, n.d.

English Standard Version Study Bible. Wheaton, IL: Crossway, 2008.

Fairbairn, Patrick. *Commentary on the Pastoral Epistles, I and II Timothy, Titus*. Grand Rapids: Zondervan, 1956.

Fee, Gordon. *1 and 2 Timothy, Titus*. New International Bible Commentary. Peabody, MA: Hendrickson, 1993.

Gill, John. *An Exposition of the New Testament*, vol. 2. London: William Hill Collingridge, 1852.

Gouge, William. *Of Domesticall Duties*. London: 1622.

Grabill, Stephen J. *Rediscovering Natural Law in Reformed Theological Ethics*. Grand Rapids: Eerdmans, 2006.

Gray, James Comper and George M. Adams. *Gray and Adams' Bible Commentary*. Vol. 5, *Romans–Revelation*. Grand Rapids: Zondervan, 1950.

Grimké, Angelina. "Letters to Catherine Beecher." In *The Feminist Papers: From Adams to deBeauvoir*, edited by Alice S. Rossi, 319–22. New York: Bantam, 1974.

Guthrie, Donald. *The Pastoral Epistles: An Introduction and Commentary*. Grand Rapids: Eerdmans, 1990.

Haller, William. *The Rise of Puritanism*. New York: Harper Torchbooks, 1957.

Harvey, H. *Commentary on the Pastoral Epistles, First and Second Timothy and Titus; and the Epistle to Philemon*. Philadelphia: American Baptist Publication Society, 1890.

Hatch, Nathan. *The Democratization of American Christianity*. New Haven: Yale University Press, 1989.

———. "The Democratization of American Christianity and the Character of American Politics." In *Taking Sides: Clashing Views in United States History*. Vol. 1, *The Colonial Period to Reconstruction*, edited by Larry Madaras and M. SoRelle, 92–101. 13th ed. Boston: McGraw-Hill Higher Education, 2009.

Heasman, Kathleen. *Evangelicals in Action: An Appraisal of Their Social Work in the Victorian Era*. London: Bles, 1962.

Helm, Paul. "Calvin and Natural Law." In *The Organizational Structure of Calvin's Theology*, edited by Richard C. Gamble, 177–94. New York: Garland, 1992.

Hendriksen, William. *Exposition of the Pastoral Epistles in New Testament Commentary*. Grand Rapids: Baker, 1957.

Henry, Matthew. *An Exposition of the Old and New Testaments*. Vol. 6, *New Testament*. London: Joseph Ogle Robinson, 1836. Online: www.biblestudytools.com/commentaries/matthew-henry-complete.

Hiebert, D. Edmund. *First Timothy*. Chicago: Moody, 1957.

Hinson, Glenn. "1–2 Timothy and Titus." In *The Broadman Bible Commentary*. Vol. 11, *2 Corinthians-Philemon*. Nashville: Broadman, 1971.

Hodge, Charles. *An Exposition of the First Epistle to the Corinthians*. Grand Rapids: Eerdmans, 1956.

Hughes, R. Kent, and Bryan Chapell. *1 and 2 Timothy and Titus: To Guard the Deposit*. Preaching the Word. Wheaton: Crossway, 2000.

Irwin, Joyce. *Womanhood in Radical Protestantism*. New York: Mellen, 1979.

Johnson, Byron. "The Good News About Evangelicalism." *First Things*, February 2011, 12–14.

Johnson, James T. "English Puritan Thought on the Ends of Marriage." *Church History* 38 (1969) 429–35.

Johnson, Paul. *A History of the American People*. New York: HarperCollins, 1997.

Kelly, Douglas F. *The Emergence of Liberty in the Modern World: The Influence of Calvin on Five Governments from the 16th Through 18th Centuries*. Phillipsburg, NJ: Presbyterian and Reformed Publishing, 1992.

Kelly, J. N. D. *A Commentary on the Pastoral Epistles, I Timothy, II Timothy, Titus*. New York: Harper & Row, 1963.

Knight, George W. III. *The Pastoral Epistles: A Commentary on the Greek Text*. Grand Rapids: Eerdmans, 1992.

———. *The Role Relationship of Men and Women: New Testament Teaching*. Chicago: Moody, 1985.

Köstenberger, Andreas J., et al., eds. *Women in the Church: A Fresh Analysis of 1 Timothy 2:9–15*. Grand Rapids: Baker, 2000.

Kroeger, Catherine Clark, and Mary J. Evans, eds. *The IVP Women's Bible Commentary*. Downers Grove, IL: InterVarsity, 2002.

Kroeger, Richard Clark, and Catherine Clark Kroeger. *I Suffer Not a Woman: Rethinking 1 Timothy 2:11–15 in Light of Ancient Evidence*. Grand Rapids: Baker, 1992.

Laslett, Peter. *The World We Have Lost: England Before the Industrial Age*. 2nd ed. New York: Scribner's, 1973.

Liddon, H. P. *Explanatory Analysis of St. Paul's First Epistle to Timothy*. Minneapolis: Klock and Klock Christian Publishers, 1897.

Longman, Tremper III and David E. Garland, eds. *Ephesians–Philemon*. Vol. 12, *The Expositor's Bible Commentary*. Rev ed. Grand Rapids: Zondervan, 2006.

Luther, Martin. "Lectures on Galatians, 1535." Vol. 26, *Luther's Works*. Edited by Jaroslav Pelikan. St. Louis: Concordia, 1963.

———. "Lectures on I Timothy." Vol. 28, *Luther's Works*. Edited by Hilton C. Oswald. St. Louis: Concordia, 1973.

———. "Temporal Authority: To What Extent It Should Be Obeyed." In *Luther's Works*, vol. 45, edited by Walther I. Brandt, 81–139. Philadelphia: Muhlenberg, 1962.

MacArthur, John Jr. *1 Timothy*. MacArthur New Testament Commentary. Chicago: Moody Press, 1995.

Macfarlane, Alan. *Marriage and Love in England: Modes of Reproduction, 1300–1840*. Oxford: Blackwell, 1986.

Manual of the Church of the Nazarene. Kansas City: Nazarene Publishing House, 1985.

McKim, Donald K., ed. *Historical Handbook of Major Biblical Interpreters*. Downers Grove, IL: InterVarsity, 1998.

Moellering, H. Armin. *1 Timothy, 2 Timothy, Titus*. Concordia Commentary. St. Louis: Concordia Publishing House, 1970.

Morgan, Edmund S. *The Puritan Family: Religion and Domestic Relations in Seventeenth-century New England*. Rev ed. New York: Harper Torchbook, 1966.

Moss, Michael C. *1, 2 Timothy and Titus*. College Press NIV Commentary. Joplin, MO: College Press, 1994.

Mounce, William D. *Pastoral Epistles*. Word Biblical Commentary. Nashville: Nelson, 2000.

Nicholson, Roy S. "I & II Timothy and Titus." Vol. 5, *The Wesleyan Bible Commentary*, edited by Charles W. Carter. Grand Rapids: Eerdmans, 1965.

Noll, Mark A. *A History of Christianity in the United States and Canada*. Grand Rapids: Eerdmans, 1992.

Novak, Michael. *On Two Wings: Humble Faith and Common Sense at the American Founding*. San Francisco: Encounter Books, 2002.

O'Connor, Lillian. *Pioneer Women Orators: Rhetoric in the Ante-Bellum Reform Movement*. New York: Columbia University Press, 1954.

Oden, Thomas C. *First and Second Timothy and Titus*. Interpretation. Louisville: John Knox, 1989.

Packer, J. I. "Understanding the Differences." In *Women, Authority, and the Bible*, edited by Alvera Mickelsen, 295–99. Downers Grove, IL: InterVarsity, 1986.

Payne, Philip B. *Man and Woman, One in Christ: An Exegetical and Theological Study of Paul's Letters*. Grand Rapids: Zondervan, 2009.

Pierce, Ronald W. and Rebecca Merrill Groothius, eds. *Discovering Biblical Equality: Complementarity Without Hierarchy*. Downers Grove, IL: InterVarsity, 2004.

Piper, John and Wayne Grudem, eds. *Rediscovering Biblical Manhood and Womanhood: A Response to Evangelical Feminism*. Wheaton: Crossway, 1991.

Poole, Matthew. *A Commentary on the Holy Bible*. Vol. 3, *Matthew-Revelation*. London: Banner of Truth, 1963.

Ryken, Leland. *Worldly Saints: The Puritans As They Really Were*. Grand Rapids: Zondervan, 1986.

Schreiner, Thomas R. "An Interpretation of I Timothy 2:9–15: A Dialogue with Scholarship." In *Women in the Church: A Fresh Analysis of 1 Timothy 2:9–15*, edited by Andreas J. Köstenberger et al., 105–54. Grand Rapids: Baker, 2000.

Scott, Thomas. *The Holy Bible, Containing the Old and New Testaments, with Explanatory Notes, Practical Observations, and Copious Marginal References*. Vol. 6. Boston: Armstrong, Crocker, and Brewster, 1831.

Smith, Page. *Daughters of the Promised Land: Women in American History*. Boston: Little, Brown, 1970.

Stark, Rodney. *The Rise of Christianity: How the Obscure, Marginal Jesus Movement Became the Dominant Religious Force in the Western World in a Few Centuries*. San Francisco: HarperSanFrancisco, 1997.

Stenton, Doris Mary. *The English Woman in History*. London: Allen & Unwin, 1957.

Stott, John. *The Message of I Timothy and Titus: God's Good News for the World*. Leicester, UK: InterVarsity, 1996.

Towner, Philip. *1—2 Timothy and Titus*. IVP New Testament Commentary. Downers Grove, IL: InterVarsity, 1994.

VanDrunen, David. *Natural Law and the Two Kingdoms: A Study in the Development of Reformed Social Thought*. Grand Rapids: Eerdmans, 2010.

Wesley, John. *Explanatory Notes Upon the New Testament*. Vol. 2, *Romans to Revelation*. Grand Rapids: Baker, 1983.

Whitby, Daniel. *A Paraphrase and Commentary on the New Testament*. Vol. 2, *The Epistles*. Rev ed. London: Bagster, 1809.

Williams, Roger. "The Bloody Tenent of Persecution, for Cause of Conscience, Discussed." In *Divine Right and Democracy: An Anthology of Political Writings in Stuart England,* edited by David Wootton, 238–47. London: Penguin, 1986.

Yarborough, Robert. "The Hermeneutics of I Timothy 2:9–15." In *Women in the Church: A Fresh Analysis of 1 Timothy 2:9–15,* edited by Andreas J. Köstenberger et al., 155–96. Grand Rapids: Baker, 2000.

www.ingramcontent.com/pod-product-compliance
Lightning Source LLC
Chambersburg PA
CBHW070930160426
43193CB00011B/1644